The Colors of Excellence

The Colors of Excellence

Hiring and Keeping Teachers of Color in Independent Schools

PEARL ROCK KANE
ALFONSO J. ORSINI

EDITORS

Teachers College
Columbia University
New York and London

Dedication

To the teachers of color in independent schools who blaze the trail to greater diversity.

And to the trustees, administrators, teachers, and parents who seek and support such change.

Published by Teachers College Press, 1234 Amsterdam Avenue, New York, NY 10027

Library of Congress Cataloging-in-Publication Data

    The colors of excellence : hiring and keeping teachers of color in independent schools / Pearl Rock Kane, Alfonso J. Orsini, editors.
      p. cm.
    Includes bibliographical references and index.
    ISBN 0-8077-4282-1 (pbk. : alk. paper)
    1. Minority teachers—Employment—United States. 2. Private schools—United States—Faculty. 3. Faculty integration—United States. I. Kane, Pearl Rock. II. Orsini, Alfonso, J.
    LB2835.25 .C65   2002
    371.02—dc21   2002-032081

ISBN 0-8077-4282-1 (paper)

Printed on acid-free paper

Manufactured in the United States of America

10 09 08 07 06 05 04   8 7 6 5 4 3

Contents

Acknowledgments

This book grew out of a study of faculty diversity in independent schools. The intended outcome is an enhanced understanding of ways that independent schools can attract and retain greater numbers of teachers of color. Many Teachers College graduate students participated in various aspects of the research. Some of their work is included in this volume, and research efforts of others provided the building blocks for the studies.

In addition to those whose work appears in this book, there are many who participated in such facets of the study as researching the literature, developing surveys, conducting interviews, analyzing the survey data, synthesizing the findings, and selecting the stories that were submitted for consideration for publication. For their important contributions, we wish to thank Jessica Bagby, Christopher D. Harrow, Marshall James, Parag Joshi, Marc Kramer, Jeremy LaCasse, Sally Mixsell, Michelle Smith, Jan Scott, Janelle Scott, Lynn Sorensen, David Suter, and Danielle Wilcox. We have a special debt to those who reviewed and commented on parts of the manuscript: Leslie Jeffs, Sally Mixsell, and David Suter. These students, most of whom are slated for administrative jobs in schools, influenced the thinking of many of their graduate school colleagues with whom they discussed their findings in the study halls and classrooms of Teachers College. We also wish to extend our sincere thanks to Carollyn R. Finegold and Beril Ulku-Steiner who helped in organizing various facets of the study and to Jane Mallison and Susan O'Hara for assistance in editing parts of the manuscript. We owe special gratitude to Ara C. Brown for his enormous assistance in all of the final stages of preparing this manuscript.

The Altman Foundation's president, Jane O'Connell, and vice president and executive director, Karen Rosa, inspired us to undertake this venture and encouraged us to take the initial study of New York City programs to a national level. Their enthusiasm sustained us, and their generous support makes this book possible.

We are grateful to the many committed teachers and administrators in independent schools who met with us, the teachers and administrators who responded to our survey, and the organizational leaders who gave us their thoughts through lengthy interviews. Our sincere hope, and the intent of the

Altman Foundation, is that this book will spark substantive conversations among teachers, administrators, students, parents, and trustees that will lead to positive changes in the culture of schools, paving the way for many people of color to build satisfying careers as teachers and administrators in independent schools.

Answering the Call

Pearl Rock Kane

Among nonsectarian schools in America, the small group of private schools that call themselves "independent schools" rank among the most prestigious educational institutions in America.[1] Financially self-supporting and largely free of government intervention, independent schools are able to define themselves, determine their own curriculum, and select faculty and students who they feel will best fit with the school's mission. Within the independent school sector, the most costly and best known are the approximately 1,100 schools affiliated with the National Association of Independent Schools (NAIS), which serve approximately 500,000 students.[2]

These schools, all of which have a demanding academic curriculum for their students, emphasize academic rigor and character development. They enjoy an influence disproportionate to their actual numbers because of the quality of their academic programs, the success their graduates have in matriculating at competitive colleges and universities, and the substantial social, economic, and political capital of their alumni.

Most independent schools have always prided themselves in preparing students to occupy leadership roles in society, but it wasn't until the Civil Rights Movement of the 1960s that independent schools began to confront their homogeneity and act on a newly awakened sense of social responsibility to educate a more diverse student body. Following on the heels of this new sense of social justice, came the reality that all graduates would be living and working in an increasingly diverse world. It took another 20 years for these schools to recognize an equally strong need to have a diverse faculty. To prepare students for leadership in a diverse society, independent schools would have to provide a microcosm of that diverse society. Thoughtful educators recognized that students of color and White students need to see role models of people of color in authority positions within schools. Interactions with teachers of color during the formative years of schooling is a necessary precondition for breaking down stereotypes White students may form about people who are different from themselves, opening the possibility of achieving greater understanding in the school and in society. In the 1990s, this growing imperative for faculty diversity came to the attention of the Altman Foundation, a small philanthropic organization in New York City with a long history of fostering school improvement.

The Altman Foundation was supporting several small programs aimed at diversifying independent schools that were meeting with only marginal success despite the efforts of their committed leaders. The resulting sense of frustration sparked the Foundation's interest in delving more deeply into the complexity of issues affecting the attraction and retention of teachers of color. Through a generous research grant awarded to the Klingenstein Center at Teachers College, Columbia University, the Altman Foundation supported a broad study designed to publicize and demystify the problem of attracting and retaining teachers of color. Their support allowed us to approach the problem from multiple perspectives and ultimately involved the efforts of 33 graduate students at Teachers College as well as collaborative research with the National Association of Independent Schools.

Empirical data for this study were collected and analyzed over a period of 5 years, but the completed study lacked an essential component—the authentic voices of teachers of color. We decided to collect stories of teachers and students of color about their own, firsthand experiences in independent schools.

To reach our intended audience, we tapped the networks of the Klingenstein Center and the National Association of Independent Schools, and contacted people via electronic communication. We invited submissions that addressed the positive and heartening rewards of life in independent schools as well as the frustrations and disappointments. "Whatever the experience," we told prospective contributors, "we want to hear about it because your story will help shed light on how independent schools can become more diverse." To encourage candor, contributors were free to use their own names or fictitious names. All chose to use their real names, although several stories contain fictitious names for people mentioned in them.

Twenty-five personal accounts by teachers were submitted for consideration. A panel of four judges read each of these and made recommendations. Ten full stories (set as sub-chapters) and excerpts from seven others were selected for inclusion in this publication. The combination of objective findings and personal stories provides the reader with a balance of "empirical" and "anecdotal" data. The study drew on the writing talents of the teachers of various races and ethnicities who submitted their stories; some were already accomplished authors, but others had not written for publication before.

We hope a frank report on the current state of diversity in independent schools, strengthened with authentic voices of several teachers of color, will foster productive dialogue on what schools might do both to increase faculty diversity and to enhance the experiences of those teachers who constitute it. If independent schools become more thoughtful and receptive environments for teachers of color, they also will become places where differences of all kinds are not only respected but valued. Independent school educators and trustees have the power to transform their schools into healthier educational environments for all constituents.

The first step in embarking on any form of change is to confront reality. These personal stories of independent school faculty provide powerful testimony of the advantages, joys, hazards, and pain experienced by teachers of color in this setting. Their authentic voices deliver a poignant message to those who are serious about changing their schools.

Since the number of teachers of color in independent schools is small, we use the term "teachers of color" to represent various races and ethnicities. Such use does not intend to suggest that people of color are a monolithic group who experience racial identity in the same way. Racial identity differs for individuals both within and across groups, and, of course, also may differ by social class. For some individuals, ethnicity or social class may be a more powerful determiner than race. (Although White racial identity is not the focus of this book, we fully recognize that White teachers can be seen as part of racial and ethnic groups. An exploration of White identity and privilege and the development of race consciousness may be a necessary precursor to the creation of more caring schools.[3]

In Chapter 1, "The Need for Teachers of Color," we discuss the demographic revolution taking place in America and try to convey the importance of teachers of color in independent schools. We describe the way in which teachers of color serve as important role models for students of color and, generally, have high expectations for them. They serve in a different way as role models for White students, preparing them to live and work in a world economy in which Whites are increasingly in the minority. We argue that a diverse teaching force is crucial to the shaping of a positive school culture.

The personal stories accompanying this chapter describe outright racism that authors Cooper and Zaloom experienced as students in independent schools. In "The Silent Years" Chad Cooper recounts that only in his senior year in college did he begin to deal with his painful experiences in an independent school. He further notes, ". . . had there been a strong African American role model with power in my school, I would have had a visible ally, and I may not have had to hold in my feelings quite so long."

In "Dirty Knees" Shafia Zaloom recalls her social problems as a Chinese American student in an independent school. Only when, in a college class, she was first assigned a piece of literature by an Asian American did she feel personally validated and empowered. She decided to return to teach in an independent school to confront issues surrounding racism and effect change. Last year a student wrote "Oppress Asians" on her board as a joke, and another student labeled her a "Fortune Cookie" in a photo exhibit of faculty; she refers to both these experiences as teachable moments that exhausted her. Zaloom calls combating racism a lifelong process: ". . . we have come far but we have miles to go."

Chapter 2, "A Context for Understanding Faculty Diversity," provides a framework for considering the challenges of recruiting teachers of color in the face of a shrinking national teaching pool. The demographic situation is complicated by the fact that, for a number of reasons, people of color are not choosing teaching. The chapter provides a brief history of diversity in independent schools, a history that indicates a trend of limited success in faculty recruitment.

The stories accompanying Chapter 2, "Gifts from the Great Spirit" by Melanie Sainz and "My Chance Encounter with Independent Schools" by Dennis Bisgaard, describe their serendipitous routes to jobs in independent schools. Bisgaard, a biracial man from Denmark, says his "interesting" experiences in independent schools have made life unnecessarily rough at times, but he appreciates the generally wonderful education such schools can provide, and he is buoyed by efforts to make the curriculum, the traditions, and the school culture more inclusive.

Sainz, a member of the Hochuk National Tribe of Wisconsin, responded to an employment advertisement in a local newspaper, although she had never heard of an "independent day school" before. Despite a rocky beginning, Sainz believes strongly enough in the independent school in which she teaches to educate her own children there. Nonetheless, she looks forward "to the day when I can take what I learned from this experience back home 'to help my people.'"

Chapter 3, "Findings from a National Survey of Teachers of Color and from Analysis of the NAIS Database," presents the findings of a national survey of 691 teachers of color concerning factors related to teacher attraction and retention: how teachers found their jobs, their reasons for choosing to teach in an independent school, the special demands on them as teachers of color, and the degree of likelihood that they will stay in independent school teaching. The survey also explores the experience of recruitment agencies in placing teachers of color and considers reasons why some schools are more diverse than others. Both stories accompanying Chapter 3, "Excess Baggage" by Alexis Wright and "Struggles and Rewards" by Reveta Bowers, contain anecdotes about the effects of stereotyping and perpetuating stereotypes—but with differing perspectives. When Wright arrived for his first job interview, he saw an African American male opening car doors for arriving children. The "doorman" turned out to be the physical education teacher. Wright points to the need for independent schools to be conscious of the ways in which appearances may be interpreted by the outside community, particularly by candidates who come for interviews. Wright is one of several authors who underscore the need for support groups for teachers of color, the kind of help he has found by attending the NAIS People of Color Conference.

Reveta Bowers, a 30-year independent school veteran who is now a head of school, tells an anecdote from her first year of teaching. One of her endearing 5-year-old students proudly issued an invitation to dinner at his home, assuring her she would love the meal: "We're going to have ribs and watermelon," he beamed. Bowers recognizes that while most independent schools have embraced the goal of becoming diverse, multicultural communities, she must still battle being stereotyped.

Chapter 4, "An Analysis of Teacher Diversity in Eleven Independent Schools," presents the findings of a field study of diversity efforts. A total of 43 interviews were conducted. Those interviewed in each school were the head of school, two teachers of color, and the person most responsible for diversity efforts at the school. The purpose was to examine each school's stated views on commitment to recruiting and retaining faculty of color and to gather evidence (or lack thereof) of that commitment. The chapter concludes by synthesizing themes that emerged from the interviews: defining diversity, commitment, support and leadership, open communication, and critical mass. Also included is a list of provocative questions for schools serious about diversity.

The existence of several of these themes—commitment, support and leadership, and open communication—may be the reason teachers Erik Resurreccion and Lisa Arrastia, whose stories accompany Chapter 4, have stayed at their respective schools, although they continue to struggle with their decision to work in independent schools. In "How Did I End Up Here?" Resurreccion explains that he stays not only for the chance to be a positive role model and an advocate for diversity issues in the school, but also because he has colleagues who have the same goals and vision for achieving equity and justice at the school.

Although alienated by her own experience as a student in an independent school, Arrastia, author of "Should I Stay or Should I Go Now?" returned to an independent school as a teacher and administrator after several years of teaching in a run-down public school. Arrastia struggles with the "cognitive dissonance" she feels as a Black Cuban teacher in an affluent independent school. She is torn between the chance to work in an entitled environment where she can teach socially relevant curriculum to privileged youngsters, and the desire to return to teach in a public school in a low-income community where students of color usually are denied access to a decent education.

Chapter 5, "Three Case Studies: The Wingate School, the Quaker School, and Heights Academy," provides portraits of three schools operating at different stages along the continuum of faculty diversification. The portraits (all of which use fictitious names) provide insights into what contributes to their relative degrees of success. "Wingate" has reached a stasis, although a new head of school understands that diversity requires a change in the culture of the school. "The Quaker School" has succeeded in bolstering lagging enrollment by diversifying the student body and simultaneously increasing the number of faculty of color. "Heights Academy," founded to reflect the dreams of Martin Luther King, Jr., is furthest along in achieving a diverse faculty and student body and in establishing a truly multicultural environment.

The stories that accompany Chapter 5, "Affirming Hispanic Co-workers in a School Community" by Susana Epstein and "The Journey of an Indian American Student and Teacher" by Pia Awal, demonstrate different levels of school engagement in diversity. Awal reflects on her experience of "being different" as a student in an independent school where, she recalls, diversity of any kind was ignored. She wonders if diversity just wasn't noticed or if the goal was to create a unified student body "who all fit into a mold." Currently a second-grade teacher in an independent school, Awal feels she has created an atmosphere for embracing diversity among her students. She has not found the same level of openness among most faculty and administrators, who seem bent on avoiding discourse about diversity.

Latina educator Susana Epstein works in a school where she was able to design a project that asked her Spanish students to use their linguistic skills to interview members of the school's Hispanic support staff. Epstein observes that staff often are treated as invisible, a phenomenon that mirrors behavior and social attitudes of the broader society. She notes that her students' interviews resulted in more respectful relations toward staff members and led to meaningful discussions on sexism, social class, racism, and cultural distinctions among Hispanics.

The final chapter, "The Challenge of Diversifying Independent Schools," contains a synthesis of the findings of this book as well as implications of taking action. We hope to leave our readers with specific suggestions on how they might begin to address the faculty diversity gap in their own schools.

Our further hope is that, taken together, these studies and personal stories will begin to form a vivid composite picture, not just of the current state of faculty diversity in American independent schools and possible improvements, but also of what it means to be a teacher of color in one of those schools.

CHAPTER 1

The Need for Teachers of Color in Independent Schools

Pearl Rock Kane and Alfonso J. Orsini

As I contemplate the difficulty of attracting teachers of color to independent schools, I think about the array of teachers of color I have befriended during my career. I wonder, "How did we all end up here?" While some came to teach in independent schools through the traditional employment route, a large percentage of us have something in common. Many of us are alumni/ae of independent schools. We returned to teach at our alma maters or another independent school. As I recall conversations with my alumni colleagues, it is clear that we all harbor a variety of memories of our individual student experiences; mostly, we all remember that there were few teachers of color for us to turn to. That fact may not have brought all of us back to the hallowed halls of independent schools, but it is, no doubt, recognized as we walk them daily.

Cordenia A. Paige
Georgetown Day School, Washington, D.C.

Independent schools have made relatively small strides in adding teach-ers of color to their faculties, despite the hard work and commitment of dedi-cated people and generous financial support from the Altman Foundation, the DeWitt Wallace/Reader's Digest Fund, and other foundations. Statistics from the National Association of Independent Schools show just over 7% of the 45,877 teachers in independent schools are people of color, whereas public schools in the United States have approximately 13% teachers of color. The figure of 7% is itself low, but it does not reflect the even gloomier fact that 27% of all independent schools responding to the NAIS annual survey had not even one teacher of color on their staff. Another 17% had only one teacher of color. (These figures are from an analysis of the database compiled in our 1997 study.)

The NAIS Statistics suggest that the percentage of teachers of color rose from 7.3 in 1997 to 8.4 in 1999 at an undetermined number of "core sample" member schools.[1] There was no breakdown of teachers of color by ethnic group in the 1999 statistics. These figures suggest the startling fact that many students graduating from independent schools have had no interaction with a teacher of color.

Despite surface advances in race relations, racial attitudes, and access to opportunity for people of color, America remains a racially divided country. In 1987 in New York, for example, 57% of the state's Black students were in intensely segregated public schools, while 85.1% of Hispanic students were in predominantly minority schools.[2] The pattern in New York prevails in other states and cities. Indeed, according to the *Digest of Education Statistics*, in 1999, nationally 48% of African American students and 75% of Hispanic stu-dents attended schools at which more than 75% of students were students of color.[3]

Other less apparent, but nonetheless significant, divisions between the races still exist. One study of Whites found that 78% consider Blacks more inclined than Whites to prefer to live on welfare; 62% thought Blacks less likely to be hard working; and 56% thought Blacks more prone to violence. Among non-Hispanics polled, 74% thought Hispanics more likely to prefer to live on welfare; 50% thought Hispanics more likely to be violence prone; and 56% thought Hispanics more likely to be lazy.[4] These responses may represent a less prejudiced view toward these groups than that held by previous genera-tions, but the survey indicates a frightening degree of confirmation of racial prejudice and misunderstanding. These and other views, as author Gerald Grant suggests, may be "kept in the closet" but are still "allowed to persist."[5]

Continuing changes in American demographics show that "White Ameri-cans are entering an era in which [they] are going to be outnumbered in at least some of the venues of daily life."[6] Since racial misconceptions and ten-sions persist in the larger world, it is all the more important that schools try harder to change people's thinking about such matters and about our relationships with each other. As author Parks-Daloz recognize, "We [will] take the first step into the 21st century when we recognize each school as a 'mini-commons' in which we all have a shared stake."[7]

What exactly is the significance of the role played by teachers of color in this "mini-commons"? A good deal has been written about the significant role of teachers of color in public schools, but no studies have yet been published on their specific significance in independent schools.

There are those of us in life who seem to always be "bridging the gap" between those who have opportunity and those who do not. I am one of those people. I find myself again in the South, but this time I am not called to march, sit-in, or demonstrate. This time I have been called to the "table" or "fight" for equal rights using more subtle techniques to help unlock closed minds and doors, to provide all students access to educational opportunities through program development in independent schools.

It is essential to have a headmaster and board who have vision and who are committed to providing equal access to qualified students regardless of race, religion, or social or economic differences. Fortunately, our school is led by a headmaster who recognizes that for the school to progress, it must open its gates wider to allow for greater diversity among students and faculty. Our school head also knows he must maintain a delicate balance between those who like the "system" just the way it is and others who want more diversity and a campus more reflective of the global world in which we actually live. I have been supported and empowered in my efforts to make a difference.

Mariah Landrum Childs
Notre Dame Academy, GA

TEACHERS OF COLOR AS ROLE MODELS

One frequently noted fact is that teachers of color are crucial as role models for students of color.[8] Their presence can prevent students of color from experiencing diminished levels of aspiration or from feeling that the entire educational endeavor is driven by White values and focused on White students.[9] The 1986 Carnegie Forum's assessment notes that the race and background of their teachers tell students something about authority and power in contemporary America. These messages influence children's attitudes toward school, their academic accomplishments, and their views of their own and others' intrinsic worth. The views they form in school about justice and fairness also influence their future citizenship.[10]

Teachers of color are important role models to White students, as they shape White students' images of what people of color can and do achieve. For White students and many students of color, teachers of color could be the only people of color they see in professional roles.

> . . . non-minority students will benefit from the opportunity to experience minority teachers. Interaction with minority teachers will result in increased familiarity with minorities and in seeing them in professional roles. This can raise aspirations in minority group children and lead to higher expectations for minority group members in others.[11]

How can we expect to change the prejudices of Americans cited in the National Opinion Research Center study if we cannot offer children vivid examples of people of color in roles of authority, wisdom, and aspiration? If teachers of color act as significant role models, they are especially significant in the independent school world, where students of color, especially scholarship students, often are separated either on a daily or a full-time boarding basis from their homes, their communities, and their cultures. In 1999–2000, 17.4% of students in NAIS schools (including schools in Hawaii and U.S. territories) were students of color.[12] For these young people of color, many of whom were studying in an upper-middle-class version of White-dominated society, the teacher of color who already has successfully negotiated such a world could be a great source of wisdom, a provider of cues for behavior, a source of inspiration, and a cultural decoder.

To gain a better sense of the economic level of independent school students, and their propensity to be economically and thus racially in one echelon, one need only consider that the majority of full-tuition-paying students at NAIS schools are from the 1.5 million families in America with after-tax incomes above $75,000.[13] Of course, we should not lose sight of the fact that teaching students of color, whether in public or independent schools, is not the exclusive responsibility of teachers of color; that is the responsibility of all teachers for all students.[14]

I grew up in the Bronx surrounded by Hispanics, Blacks, and other minorities, and suddenly I found myself living and teaching in an area that was predominantly White. I was not prepared to enter such an affluent community after living in a poor area of New York City for so many years. Nor was I prepared for the mind-set I encountered. To introduce myself to my students, I mentioned that I came to the United States from the Dominican Republic, and I proceeded to ask them if anyone knew where the Dominican Republic was. Only one student in my classes was able to identify the Dominican Republic on a map. When I asked if anyone knew any Hispanics and which countries they came from, students responded: "My gardener is Mexican." "The woman who cleans my house is from Venezuela." "My nanny is from Argentina, I think." I wanted someone to say, "My doctor is from the Dominican Republic," or, "The woman who works with my mom is from Argentina." That first day I learned that I had to be a lot more than just the Spanish teacher; I had to be a Hispanic role model as well.

Victoria Vlad
The Shipley School, PA

TEACHERS OF COLOR AS SHAPERS OF SCHOOL CULTURE, VALUES, AND POLICY

Since a school's culture and values, as well as its curriculum, are largely shaped by the administrators and teachers, a diverse teaching force is crucial. Much of teaching is autobiographical; we teach who we are.

The teachers who promote the culture and values of the school tend to do that through their own experience. If . . . teachers do not fully represent our rapidly changing . . . school population, then all children may very well miss an equitable education and will not be exposed to a wealth of diverse images in authority and teaching roles.[15]

Author Mary Dilworth confirms the ability of teachers of color to affect formation of educational policy and experience.

> Given their culturally diverse backgrounds and academic training defined by the White majority, Black, Hispanic, and other minority teachers possess a consummate understanding of the relationship between education and the society. This knowledge enhances the quality of education when these teachers offer students broader and more complex interpretations of the educational curriculum, and where they translate and interpret for their majority peers, in educational terms, the cultural backgrounds of their students.[16]

Dilworth's analysis notes that teachers of color in independent schools have themselves navigated both a majority and a minority culture and thus are crucial guides and interpreters for others. They can help change White values and White notions of pedagogy and thus aid the transition to culturally responsive pedagogy suitable for the new America. As Dilworth notes, an "awareness of their own experience and the experience of the dominant culture of the educational system . . . creates a cross-cultural awareness that can provide a rich knowledge base for teaching and learning in multicultural contexts."[17]

Not only traditional attitudes but some traditional pedagogical techniques may need changing. Professor Lisa Delpit and others have begun to question the efficacy for students of color of techniques, such as the open classroom and process writing, designed and administered by Whites. Delpit concludes that veteran Black teachers with intimate, firsthand knowledge of and respect for Black students' cultural backgrounds, may have had much more success in using traditional methods to teach Black children than did their liberal White counterparts using progressive techniques.[18] Incorporation of new methods suggested by the National Council of Teachers of Mathematics (NCTM) in four urban junior high schools has been found to diminish "African American students' opportunities to understand, communicate and apply mathematical ideas," because the methods were not culturally responsive.[19] In another essay, Delpit chronicles the White pedagogical power structure and its reluctance to incorporate the cultural knowledge of Black students and teachers.[20] In a similar vein, Gloria Ladson-Billings, in *The Dreamkeepers*, chronicles the views and techniques of eight teachers (three White, five Black) who have been particularly successful with African American students.[21] The critical ingredients to the teachers' success seem to be an understanding of and respect for culture and culturally relevant teaching. Faculties that include culturally diverse points of view and values are important. This is especially true since a thorough understanding of different cultures and culturally relevant pedagogy is not widely taught in colleges and schools of education. Exposure to new ways of seeing things is important for public schools, but perhaps even more important for independent schools, which may be steeped in White, upper-middle-class traditions of culture and education. This searching for knowledge of various traditions significantly helps to define and focus independent schools' missions. Teachers increasingly will be asked to be cognizant of cultural variations in behavioral, communication, and learning styles in order to create culturally compatible classrooms.[22] The presence of teachers of color, especially in independent schools, will be crucial in this regard.

I often get chided by colleagues from previous jobs. Attitudes that I had "sold out," by leaving the public sector for a private school. Some believe I must work in a dream situation where ALL children are smart, motivated, and well behaved. Well, children are children and they come to me with a wide range of academic abilities. Some of my kindergartners read as well as second graders; others need help to learn the alphabet. Some are doing double-column addition and subtraction; others struggle just to write their numerals. And while no child comes to my school hungry or returns home to an empty house—because both parents work and still they cannot afford to pay a baby-sitter with their low wages—many children in my class miss daily contact and support from their mommies and daddies because they work long hours or are seemingly always away on a business or vacation trip. It is not uncommon to know a nanny a lot better than a child's parents, whom I rarely see. Many children in independent schools need the very same kinds of support and nurturing as children in public schools, but I also bring another element into their experience.

Kay Garth-Lee
Polytechnic School, CA

STUDIES ON STUDENT/TEACHER INTERACTION BY RACE

The most significant argument for the importance of teachers of color is the nature of their interaction with students in the classroom based on race.[23] Researchers Beady and Hansell found that while Black and White teachers did not differ in their perceptions of Black students' current achievement and effort, they did differ in their expectations for Black students' future success.[24]

Black teachers expected their Black students to be more successful in college than did White teachers. Since research by Kash and Borich concludes that the self-concepts of children are significantly affected by their perceptions of how teachers regard them, these higher expectations by teachers of color become particularly important to the success of students of color.[25] Other studies emphasize this point by concluding that low teacher expectations can have a more negative effect on African American students than on White students.[26]

Telling research also has been conducted regarding patterns of verbal and nonverbal communication in interracial student/teacher interactions. Experiments were conducted in which White subjects (teachers) with high and low degrees of racial prejudice were led to offer scripted praise to Black and White students. While the verbal responses of the White high-prejudice teachers were scripted, they nevertheless showed discriminatory nonverbal behavior. In a second experiment, both White and Black teachers were found to show more positive nonverbal behavior toward students of their own race.[27]

A study of eight White and eight Black, female, first-grade teachers in the urban public school setting assessed differences in verbal communication based on the gender and race of child and race of teacher.[28] The findings show that "White teachers directed more verbal praise and criticism and non-verbal praise toward males and more non-verbal criticism toward Black males."[29] Washington examined White and Black teachers' perceptions of and behavior toward White and Black second-grade children in reading groups. She found that White teachers viewed Black children more negatively, and Black teachers had perceptions of Black children that were at the midpoint, neither positive nor negative. Washington also concluded that White teachers were "clearly more positive and Black teachers clearly less positive in their behavior toward Afro-American children than their attitude scores would suggest."[30] She cites an overcompensation effect as a possible source of the behavior, with the rationale that White teachers may try to mask their cultural differences and negative attitudes, while Black teachers may be compelling their Black students to achieve in a world known to be difficult.

Holliday found that even when teacher behavior is not negative, teacher attitudes toward low- and moderate-income Black students may affect student achievement. Her study concluded that children's self-perceptions (locus of control, self-esteem) do not correlate with achievement as measured in reading and math scores. On the other hand, teacher perceptions are interdependent with and significantly related to children's achievement as measured by the same means. Teacher attitudes (perspectives based on outside experience) "have a stronger direct effect on children's achievement than both the children's self-perceptions and the . . . teachers' perceptions of children's behavioral competence."[31]

The established evidence of teachers' differential attitudes and behaviors based on race shows that teachers of color are a needed presence in all schools to help their White colleagues question their attitudes and reflect on their behavior toward students. This is especially true at independent schools, because of their cultural and geographical isolation from the cultures of students of color. Teachers of color can be a crucial force in elevating institutional understanding and changing behavior nationally at the institutional and classroom level. More recent research has focused on broadening understanding of different learning and cognitive styles among multicultural populations.[32] Teachers of color bring firsthand experience of the view of White culture from the margins of society, a view their White colleagues and students otherwise may lack. The selective and rather elite world of independent schools is surrounded by extremely wide margins.

———————

When I decided to teach at Penn Charter, my father advised me that the best way to contribute to change is from within the organization rather than from the outside. As I gained confidence at Penn Charter School, I became involved in the life of the school beyond my classroom. I accepted the job of curriculum coordinator in the middle school. I also served on an intensive summer task force that contributed to the school's educational strategic plan. I served on the school-wide curriculum committee as a representative of the middle school. I became co-coordinator of diversity. Currently, I write two columns in the school's professional newsletter, a diversity column entitled "Mosaic," and a column for the Writing Center. This past summer, in conjunction with the other diversity coordinator, I began a summer enrichment program for students, some of whom are new to Penn Charter and some who are continuing their education but need extra support. Many of these students are African American, and we hope that our daily work with them and our weekly meetings with their families will contribute to greater academic success in the upcoming school year. I have asked for more and more responsibility from the leadership of my school, and it usually has been granted.

I've learned that there is no particular entitlement that comes with being a person of color. I have never felt that I did the school a favor by being on the faculty or that the school owed me anything except professional opportunity. I acquired a sound work ethic and patience from my parents, and I have worked hard to

show that I can handle the responsibility given to me. My father
was right when he said to me that I could make more of a difference from the "inside" than from the "outside."

Cheryl Irving
William Penn Charter School, PA

ADVICE FROM THE EXPERTS

Over the past decade, a number of programs have emerged to recruit teachers
of color for independent schools and to provide teachers of color with external support in the beginning years of their career. Eight prominent people leading such efforts were invited for personal interviews.[33] The purpose was to glean
their wisdom and experience with the intention of disseminating the findings
to the wider educational community. Using a loosely-structured interview format, interviewees were asked to share the "most important lessons learned about
what contributes to success in attracting and retaining teachers of color."[34]

The collective wisdom of these respondents called for school-wide change,
the need for schools truly attempting to recruit and retain faculty to make an
institutional commitment to diversity. Schools succeeding in diversifying their
faculty have embarked on systemic change that involves all of the school constituents and scrutinizes every aspect of school life. They talked about the need
for educating trustees, administrators, teachers, staff, students, and parents, for
reviewing the curriculum to insure inclusion of non-Western thinkers and for
examining the nature of extracurricular activities, as well as access to and participation in them. Institutional change meant educating the entire community about
race, not just helping people of color accommodate to the school. Diversification focused on working with the "majority." As one leader stated, "The culture
of the school has to change, otherwise you have lip service and a revolving door."

A second theme that emerged from these interviews with organizational
leaders focused on political dynamics and the need to identify "power centers" in schools; indeed, change requires "getting a handle on where the power
lies." If the board or the parent body are controlling the school on matters of
diversity, then that group must be fully apprised and in agreement about where
the school is headed, and they must be encouraged to make their sentiments
public. Otherwise, the school will be hampered in its efforts.

One of the most informative interviews was conducted with Rachel
Conescu of the DeWitt Wallace Foundation. Between 1988 and 1998, the
DeWitt Wallace Foundation invested $12 million in the Independent School

Opportunity Program (ISOP) which was designed specifically to bring racial diversity to independent schools. The Foundation offered schools multi-year grants of $200,000 to $400,000. Independent schools used the funds toward financial aid for student scholarships, for increasing the number of faculty of color, or for collaborative ventures with other schools or organizations that were designed to increase and support diversity. In 1998, 78 representatives from 37 schools that received DeWitt Wallace Foundation funding met to pool their thinking on strategies for recruiting, hiring, and retaining faculty of color in independent schools. The outcome of the meeting resulted in recommendations of concrete steps that schools might take to increase the likelihood of recruiting and retaining faculty of color. These recommendations are delineated in the following sections.

Recruiting Faculty of Color

- Start early
- Create an action plan: delineate goals, course of action, develop a timetable
- Review progress regularly
- Inform the entire school community of the plan and its progress
- Pursue people identified throughout the year, even before specific openings become available
- Find creative ways to capitalize on the talents of people of color to strengthen the faculty
- Join with independent schools in the region to strengthen recruitment efforts and pool resources for recruitment
- Set up a pro-active recruitment team
- Allow the head of school to work directly with chairs of departments and division directors
- A hiring committee should be supervised by a single individual, accountable for coordinating all recruitment efforts
- Include representatives from each level of the school, students and board members
- Expand the recruitment network to include:
  - Alumni, teachers, and parents
  - Local colleges and universities—target specific academic departments, clubs, and organizations
  - Historically black colleges and universities
  - Local and national job fairs
  - Recruitment agencies and consortia that target people of color
  - Non-profit organizations such as local churches, community based organizations, the NAACP, the United Negro College Fund, and the Urban League

- Business contacts as a source for candidates considering new career options.

Hiring Policies and Practices for Faculty of Color

- Involve the entire school community in creating a hiring policy
- The Board of trustees must state their commitment to a diverse faculty, which should be reflected in the school's mission statement and strategic plan
- The faculty and parents should help the school head define long- and short-term hiring goals, minimum job qualifications, and specific selection criteria
- A hiring committee should reflect the diversity the school is seeking to create and include students, faculty, and staff from each level of the school
- Train committee members through role plays, case studies, and simulations
- Familiarize the committee with NAIS hiring guidelines
- Charge the committee with conducting interviews and authorize the committee to make final recommendations to the head of school
- Conduct effective interviews
- Interview strong candidates even if there are no immediate job openings
- Get feedback by conducting exit interviews from faculty leaving the school and candidates who turn down an offer
- Allow candidates an honest look at what is happening at the school
- Enable candidates to meet alone with faculty of color
- Carefully review job descriptions and articulate the breadth of the roles candidates will need to play
- Clarify the perks associated with teaching in independent schools that offset relatively low salaries, and describe other structures, such as mentoring/internship programs, that may appeal to candidates
- Evaluate a candidate's "intangible" assets in addition to degrees, experience, and pedagogical skills, discuss what it means to be "qualified"

Retaining Faculty of Color

- Keep careful records of how the school is progressing in its goals to diversify
- Review turnover of teachers of color over a ten-year period and reasons for teachers departing
- Consider workload/salaries/rate of promotions compared to all faculty; percentages in senior level administrative positions
- Consider which departments have the most faculty of color and why
- Review the school's mission statement and long-range and strategic plans with the entire school community—teachers, parents, and board. Is there a diversity plan? What criteria are to be used for evaluating its success?
- Review all school literature. How clearly does the school communicate its desire to be an inclusive institution?

- Conduct frank conversations with all faculty about the necessity for
  - promoting diversity; the ways diversity is manifested at the school, the amount of ethnic/racial tension on campus and the degree to which increased diversity increases or defuses racial tension
- Develop formal criteria to analyze the progress of those responsible for diversity work. Evaluate their success and seek ways to increase their productivity
- Ask alumni of color to return to school to discuss their experiences in the school. Discuss the school's progress over the years
- Build support structures
- Create affinity groups for parents and faculty of color in addition to school-wide diversity committees
- Include board members of color in these groups
- Develop mentoring programs for new teachers of color with little or no teaching experience
- Assume active interest in the welfare of teachers of color by encouraging their professional development and promoting talented individuals quickly
- Provide those responsible for diversity work with direct access to senior administrators and clearly-defined job responsibilities
- Set aside funding for programs
- Promote school-wide anti-bias training for entire community—school head and board, administrators, teachers, parents, and students
- Training should be on-going and eventually include all faculty
- Invite professional consultants to conduct workshops on diversity related issues
- Invite prominent individuals of color to speak at school assemblies
- Encourage teachers of color to attend professional conferences and institutes, especially during the summer
- Encourage graduate study or other avenues for teachers to further their own professional development and to increase commitment to remaining in education

THE SIGNIFICANCE OF TEACHERS OF COLOR AT INDEPENDENT SCHOOLS

In 1987, at 12 years old, I left the island-nations of Trinidad and Tobago for eighth grade at an independent school in New Jersey. The first day of school was so overwhelming because I had to adjust to the new faces, new accents, and new academic demands. My mother wanted me to wear a suit because the dress code description failed to suggest what we COULD wear. So I sat in my eighth-grade earth science class, shirt tightly tucked in, fidgety fingers and book bag overflowing. I was impressed by how the other students were dressed, for they seemed to navigate the dress code with finesse and chic. They wore, what I later came to recognize as the staple prep school attire, J. Crew, the Gap, and L.L. Bean. I later tried to alter my closet to mesh with my peers; the only problem was that I rarely could afford the entire ensemble. I sadly settled for mix and match pieces which at the time made me feel more marginal, more out-of-place.

In that first class, I sat mixed with anxiety and awe. I was frightened that I was the only Black person in the room, from Orange not Short Hills, who occasionally rode public transportation to school. It is hard to explain why I perennially felt uncomfortable at school, but I think it had a lot to do with my feeling like I never fit in. I always wanted to be part of the cool social cliques but never quite made it into the inside. I came close a couple of times, but most of my classmates bonded over geography or class or previously established extracurricular social networks. Since most of my classmates lived far away, I rarely could attend parties or bar mitzvahs in their neighborhoods. And if these cliques were not based on neighborhood difference, then it was based on something more ephemeral and intangible like who was pretty or had the best body or who had access to alcohol or who was the most rebellious. In some ways these are typical high school categories, but in my case I felt that no matter how hard I worked I could not change the very real presence of my racial and class difference.

It was at the Academy that I learned how to critically write and read literature. I was exposed to varsity girls' soccer and track. I experienced precious lessons on diversity awareness and cultural difference. And I was more than academically prepared for the academic demands of my college.

In my high school, I developed much closer bonds with the teachers than with many of the students. My high school English teacher made me feel more comfortable there by using literature to connect to the students of color. I remember one incident when my tenth-grade English teacher taught us Mark Twain's *Huckleberry Finn*. As we neared the finish of the book, he asked us if we thought that the book was racist, and at the time, I did not have the language to support my feeling that it was. He said that he thought the book was racist, not simply because of its diction, but rather because of the ending in which the slave, Jim, has to be given his freedom rather than locating his freedom in his escape. This class stands out because that teacher articulated racism when most of my peers felt comfortable with the inequality in the story. In those moments, I felt more comfortable discussing discrimination and exclusion. And, although I think my experience at the Academy would have been drastically better if the only other African Americans were not simply our kitchen staff, but part of the teaching staff, I felt an affinity for those English teachers who were committed to diversity.

Sal Tillet
Alumna, Newark Academy, NJ

Independent schools, which frequently pride themselves on preparing students for leadership, must recognize the need for teachers of color if they wish to prepare students to live, work, and lead in a diverse society. A search of the literature reveals few articles touching upon the need for teachers of color in independent schools. In 1971, Cora Presley, then a senior at Milton Academy, wrote of her experiences, asserting that the presence of Black adults on campus or nearby "can help to negate the feelings of dissociation that Black boarders feel."[35] She also pointed out the significance of a Black faculty member in her life as advisor and "defender." In 1993, Josh Edelman, a first-year teacher of color at Milton, chronicled his own disappointments and victories and called upon the trustees and administration of Milton Academy to create a multicultural environment "where ethnic pride is understood by all not as racist but as necessary," by hiring "new faculty of color and increasing the number of students of color."[36] In short, aside from a few eloquent essays, no comprehensive studies have been done on the need for, or the experience of, teachers of color at independent schools.

The Silent Years

Chad Cooper

Alumnus of St. Martin's Episcopal, LA

In the spring of 1989, I stood before the student body and parents as the next president of the student council. It was the year-ending awards ceremony, and it was to culminate in the outgoing student council president's transferring the "Light of St. Martin's" to me, the incoming president. By the end of my junior year, it appeared I had everything going my way. I was winner of the O.E. Haring Memorial Scholarship, which was awarded to the junior who best exhibited leadership skills. I was going to be president of the Acoloyte Club, an organization of religion students who served as altar boys and girls during chapel services. I was elected captain of the football and baseball teams for my senior year as well as student body president. I was also one year from graduating and becoming the first African American student to ever complete 12 years at St. Martin's Episcopal School, a predominantly White, private preparatory day school located in Metairie, Louisiana, a suburb of New Orleans.

As I stood before students, parents, my family, and friends during the awards ceremony, I felt so proud of my accomplishments. However, although I had achieved great political, social, and athletic success at the school, I also had encountered countless acts of racism and ignorant behavior during my time there, not only from my peers, but also from teachers.

In 12 years of attendance at St. Martin's, I never had an African American teacher, and I do not recall having a Hispanic one. The biggest influences from African American adults at the school were Larry Panna, director of the print shop and middle school basketball coach, and the vast assortment of Black janitors, the most influential on all students being Clarence Smith. Clarence was a janitor in the athletic department and watched many children grow from babies to adults, from lower school physical education through high school varsity athletics. Like Clarence, Larry was beloved by many of the students, including me. Both of these men went beyond their job titles and showed genuine concern, caring, and love for all the students at the school. These two men were loved by the students and had a strong influence on them. However, there was no African American representation on the St. Martin's academic faculty—a position that would have gone beyond traditional Black roles in the eyes of the White and Black students and would have commanded more power and respect in the eyes of the White students and faculty. Having someone in this position may have helped to teach the faculty and students racial tolerance and helped to provide African American students a person with whom to talk about such issues.

Because there were no African American teachers, I felt powerless when confronted with racism in the academic context. There was no one at the school with any power with whom I could discuss these issues. So I let them tear me down inside. I felt the most powerless when I faced actual racism and ignorance from teachers, because while I grew to expect such behavior from my peers, the behavior from teachers was unexpected and validated it in the eyes of others. And there seemed to be no remedy.

I was in lower school in the late 1970s and early 1980s. Elementary school was a slight culture shock for me, having gone from my all-Black neighborhood to my all-White school. Part of the lower school curriculum was music class. In the class, taught by Mr. Fields (fictitious name), we would sing, play instruments, and talk about music. It was a fun class.

I recall an incident in the class where we were having a discussion about music and cultures. It may have been second or third grade. During the discussion, Mr. Fields made a comment to the class that Black people liked to play drums and they listened to music on the radio all the time. He then looked to me for validation, "Isn't that right, Chad?" A young child with older siblings who did like listening to the radio, I gave the teacher his validation by smiling and nodding uncomfortably.

I was too young at the time to realize what his comments meant, but I knew even then that something in them wasn't right. As I grew older, I would wonder what impact those and similar comments from teachers and parents would have on my relationships with my peers and the way they viewed me.

During my sophomore year at St. Martin's, civics was the social studies requirement. The civics teacher was Ms. Jowett (fictitious name), a middle-aged White woman who was extremely popular among the students. But I used to hate the bell that ended third period because I knew that in 5 minutes I would have to make the walk down the long upper school corridor to Ms. Jowett's room. Whenever there was an issue of race, she would use me as an example. It was not the kind of example where she would ask my opinion or ask me to relate an experience or my perspective. She coldly made examples out of me as though I were a filmstrip or a prop to be used to better illustrate to the White kids how society really worked.

I sat nervously one particular day as Ms. Jowett was giving a lecture on the Civil Rights Movement. I prayed that the 40-minute class period would fly by, but it seemed as though the long hand on the clock was standing still. I quietly sat taking notes at my desk with my head down and my eyes looking everywhere but at the teacher, as students do when they do not want to be called upon. As she discussed how African Americans had no civil rights in the White-dominated society, she looked to me, the good Black boy, to make her point more realistic to the rest of the class. And horribly realistic to me.

The teacher asked me to walk to the front of the classroom. My trembling legs carried my solid football-player frame from my desk in the back row of the large room to stand before my classmates. What was she going to do to me this time? My brown eyes were begging for help from my fellow students as curiosity held them in their chairs. "This is how Black people were treated back then." With those words, her heavy White hand tightly gripped my forearm, and it proceeded to attempt to drag me around the room. She told the class, "This is what happens when you have no rights." She then began to throw orders at me as if I were a slave. I believe she wanted me to do as I was told. All I could do was carry my humiliated body back to the rear of the class and slide into the desk where I was taking notes. The class ended shortly thereafter. I did not tell anyone about what happened that day because I figured that she was the teacher and whatever she did in the classroom was right. She made me feel as though I were nothing, like my people were nothing. Unfortunately, I said nothing.

My silence gripped me once again as a senior. As president of the student body, I had as one of my duties to be a student representative to the disciplinary committee. This was a position of honor for a student. The committee was made up of the student body president and vice-president and several faculty members.

One case that came before us was one where two freshman White boys drew a picture of Klansmen looking down a well, presumably at an African American whom they had tossed into it. The boys then gave that drawing to an African American freshman girl. She immediately turned them in and the case came to us.

The committee heard the case from all the students and then, after letting the students leave, we began to discuss it ourselves. During the course of the discussion, Mr. Sloane (fictitious name), the faculty head of the committee, was to decide whether there was a pattern of racist behavior with these boys. He stated to the committee that if there was no pattern, then this isolated incident could be considered a "nigger joke." After he said that, not one of the White adults in the room said a thing. Neither did I. The boys were suspended.

As a student at St. Martin's, I did what many African American students in my situation do: I either pretended that I did not hear racist comments when they were made or I simply chuckled and laughed them off as not serious. In college, I began to confront these issues within myself and discuss them with others. I realized that holding in the experiences and the pain associated with them was incredibly destructive.

I was silent about racial issues and racism until my sophomore year in college, which came 3 years after St. Martin's, and it was not until my senior year in college that I began to gain some perspective on my experiences. I wrote my senior thesis based primarily on my experiences inside and outside the classroom, and I confronted some of my former classmates toward whom I had been carrying a lot of pain and anger. I realized that as my classmates grew up, so did I. I realized that I do not have to tolerate ignorance and racism, and my classmates realized that things that they said to me were wrong. Most important, I have realized that had there been a strong African American role model with power in my school, I would have had a visible ally, and I may not have had to hold in my feelings quite so long. If independent schools are going to serve students of color, they will have to hire teachers of color.

Dirty Knees

Shafia Zaloom
Presidio Hill School, CA

I am 7 and two little girls are singing to me: "Chinese, Japanese, dirty knees, look at these!" They pull the tops of their blouses into two little tent shapes to mimic small breasts and fall into each other giggling uncontrollably. I stare, silent, and feel confused and sad. "Come on," they say, "Chinese, Japanese, dirty knees, look at these!" I realize that they want me to play. I join in, "Chinese, Japanese . . . ," and laugh, feeling relieved that I have made new friends.

I am 12 and Mrs. Clark comes to my desk after class. She touches my shoulder lightly and offers me a book. There is a Chinese woman on the cover and a dragon wrapped around a pole that stands next to her. Mrs. Clark says, "I think it's important that you read this." I stay up late and ignore parent directives to go to bed so that I can read *The Woman Warrior* by Maxine Hong Kingston in 3 days. A teacher has acknowledged my difference. The book speaks volumes to me. I feel that I am not alone, but as I walk the hallways at school the next day I realize, more than ever, that I am very much alone.

I am 14 and my mother is furious when I come home for Thanksgiving vacation. At our first dinner together in 3 months, I refuse to use chopsticks because I have "forgotten how." Shaking her head as we eat, Mom is even more frustrated that I can't tolerate the spice of her cooking. I eat mostly rice, not the favorite dishes she's prepared in celebration of my first night home.

I am 15 and everyone around me seems to be dating and getting involved with boys. I remember something I heard in the neighborhood when I was younger: Chinese people are uuhhhg-ly, so I tape pictures of Christie Brinkley and Cindy Crawford on my dorm room walls and aspire to achieve perfection. I can't change the color of my skin and the shape of my eyes, but I can definitely mold and shape my body; that at least will compensate for my race. Why can't I just look more like my dad? He has green eyes. Or my grandmother—she has blue eyes AND blonde hair. I flirt with an eating disorder for a few years, but never quite cross over into the danger zone.

I am 17 and at a table with 12 students in the dining hall. Jeff tells a racist joke and the entire table laughs. I sit in silence, enraged. Later in the girl's bathroom I casually comment to Sally on Jeff's rudeness. She turns to me and says, "Don't worry about it. We don't think of *you* that way."

I am 19 and Michael is my dream come true. We are instantly close and intimate friends. We spend hours together sharing secrets and dreams. There is a chemistry between us and we start moving toward romance. Michael is resistant for months and then suddenly wants to be a couple. After a year and a half we are in a deep relationship and true love. I venture to ask what was really going on for him and why he was so apprehensive in the beginning. There is a loaded silence, and I push for more. Michael breaks down in tears and confesses that he didn't feel right dating me because I am Asian.

I am 21 and enrolled in a women's literature course where I read the first piece of literature in my entire education by an Asian American, Amy Tan. As with *Warrior*, I connect with the book and read it in a 6-hour sitting. I feel strength in the clarity I gain and empowerment in the validation I feel. As we discuss the book in class, a question about Chinese culture comes up. All eyes turn to me and expect my answer. For the first time in my life, I am expected to speak for my race. How little I feel I know.

I am 25 and new to the independent school community. Everyone keeps mixing up the three new (and only) Asian teachers on campus. We look nothing alike. For 2 years we continually have our identities confused by parents and students. We receive each other's mail and messages. Our names are switched in school publications.

I am 29 and passionate about teaching. As a biracial woman who grew up in independent schools, I ask myself why I choose to teach in one, serve on the board, and plan to make independent school teaching a career.

It wasn't until after college and my short career as a social worker, that I was able to see not only how limited my experience had been, but how little I had seen of myself reflected in the community I loved so much. In an independent school, I have worked to understand my pain and the detriment to my self-esteem that was also a result of being a kid of color who attended an independent school. As a teacher I work to confront issues of racism and effect change. Discussions of race are difficult and the work is draining.

Last year when a student wrote "Oppress Asians" on my chalkboard as a joke and another labeled me as a "Fortune Cookie" in her photo exhibit of faculty, I walked away from each of those "teachable moments" with complete and total exhaustion. I thought I didn't ever want to have another conversation about race again, but I recognize the issue is far too important. Combating racism is a lifelong process for all of us and we can't stop now; we have come far but have miles to go.

I think about Sarah and Olivia in second grade. In my work as the diversity coordinator at my alma mater grade school, while describing the concept of affinity groups to Sarah and Olivia's class, both children raised their hands and shared in loud and proud voices: "I'm Chinese!" (Sarah); "I'm Korean!" (Olivia).

Olivia and Sarah deserve to know who they are and to feel safe and valued within the school community. They and their White classmates deserve an inclusive education that will empower them to embrace their own individuality and help them to live and work in a diverse society. We sometimes must engage in difficult conversations about race. Schools can't only create space for people of color; they must empower them to move from the margins to the center. Then and only then will independent schools fulfill their mission of providing a sound education for all their children.

CHAPTER 2

A Context for Understanding Faculty Diversity

Alfonso J. Orsini

Just as there is much relevance to talk about race in America generally, there has been perhaps even greater fear among independent school people to broach the topic of faculty and student diversity, an issue that puts in question the very nature and existence of independent schools in the context of a pluralistic society. Thus, very little has been written on this topic. However, despite the paucity of published studies on the specific subject of recruitment of teachers of color at independent schools, there is much good information that can form a contextual base from which to discuss the topic.

THE DEMOGRAPHIC CONTEXT OF TEACHER DIVERSITY

The National Demographic Picture

People of color grew in number from approximately 19% of the U.S. population in 1980 to approximately 26% of the population in 1996, about 2% every 5 years, When we began this research in 1996, people of color were projected to increase to just over 28% of the population in the year 2000, and they do indeed constitute 29% of the population in the year 2002.[1] Most recent Census Bureau figures project that people of color will constitute 33% of the population by 2010, 39% by 2025 and 48% by 2050.[2] In the year 2000 people of color already constituted 41% of the population in California, 37% in Lousiana, 33% in New York, and 30% in Texas.[3]

Race and Ethnicity of Children

Leaders of public and independent schools need to be aware of the even more striking increase in diversity that will occur nationally among children ages 5–17 in the coming years, as Table 2.1 suggests.

As the diversity of children ages 5–17 increases, so too will the diversity of our nation's classrooms. What will be the full effect of that increase? Even in 1986–87, when the national percentage of children of color was 28, students of color composed 78.7% of the total population of 932,343 students in New York City public schools.[4] Similarly, in 1986, 52% of the 600,000 students in the Los Angeles Unified School District were Hispanic.[5] Spellman pointed out in 1988 that of the 5 million students in the nation's 32 largest school districts, 75% were students of color.[6] In 1993, in central cities throughout America, 32.9% of students in first through twelfth grades were African American and 21.6% were Hispanic.[7] In 1996, in central cities, 31.9% of students in first through twelfth grades were African American, and 24.3% were Hispanic.[8] Thus, as the diversity of school-aged populations increases nationally, it increases even more in the public schools of our metropolitan centers.

Suburban Diversity

The diversification of America is not limited to cities. Writer Ann Bradley cites Bellevue, Washington, a suburb of Seattle, where the percentage of students of color increased from 8 to 21 between 1981 and 1991. Similarly, between 1987 and 1991, students of color grew from 18.5% to 28.2% of the student population in the Fairfax County, Virginia, public schools. In Montgomery County, Maryland, students of color compose more than 38% of the public school population. In Glendale, California, a suburb of Los Angeles, 49% of

Table 2.1. Percentages of Children, Ages 5–17, by Race/Ethnicity Beginning in 1996 and Projected to 2025.

	1996	2000	2005	2010	2025
White	67.0	64.0	62.1	59.0	53.2
Black	14.7	14.8	15.1	15.3	15.7
Hispanic	13.2	15.1	16.8	18.4	23.0
Asian/Pacific Islander	3.6	4.2	4.9	5.5	6.9
Native American	1.0	0.9	0.9	1.0	1.0
Total Children of Color	32.5	35.0	37.7	40.2	46.6

Source: U.S. Census Bureau. (1996). *Statistical abstract of the United States*, Tables 22, 24, pp. 24, 25.

the students are non-native English speakers. Finally, Bradley cites the example of Middlesex County, New Jersey, a suburb of New York City, which has 23% students of color. Thus, the diversification of America extends beyond cities, a fact to be noted by leaders of suburban public and independent schools, who may not have recognized that hiring of teachers of color will soon be a central issue.[9]

Census Bureau data on the income levels of various racial and ethnic groups would seem to coincide with the increase in suburban diversity, inasmuch as it is axiomatic that with increased prosperity Americans have tended to seek the greener setting of the suburbs. Between 1980 and 1995, the percentage of African American families with incomes over $50,000 rose from 16.8 to 21.2,[10] and in 1999, 31.4% of Black families attained an income of over $50,000.[11] This figure still lags behind that of White families in the over $50,000 range, which rose from 36.6% in 1980 to 39.4% in 1995, and to 51% in 1999.[12] However, the increase for African Americans in percentage is larger. Furthermore, in 1995, 18.8% of Hispanic families were in the $50,000 or above income range,[13] reaching 28.7% in 1999, while 46.2% of Asian/Pacific Islander families were in the $50,000 or above range[14] in 1995, increasing to 55.6% in 1999. It bears further consideration by independent school leaders to determine whether these more than 5 million families of color in the over $50,000 range represent an increasingly diverse market for independent schools. As we will note later, Asians, who among people of color represent the highest percentage of families in the $50,000 or above range, also constitute the highest percentage of students of color in independent schools.

THE NATIONAL POOL OF TEACHERS OF COLOR

The Shrinking Teacher Force

Given the number of teachers who will be reaching retirement age in the coming decades and the projected increases in numbers of students, America stands to need more than two million new teachers in the coming decade.[15] Citing the Schools and Staffing Survey, 1993–94, Darling-Hammond astutely reminds us that among White teachers currently employed, 30% have more than 20 years on the job, while 35.3% of the Black non-Hispanic teachers, 17.1% of the Hispanic teachers, and 26.2% of Asian/Pacific Islander teachers have reached the same 20-year milestone.[16] Indeed, "a greater percentage of teachers have held their current position for twenty years or more than at any other time in the past thirty years."[17] Of course, educational policy makers and institutional leaders are rightly concerned that if schools, colleges, and departments of education are not more successful in their efforts to recruit young people of color into their ranks, the disparity between students and teachers of color in primary and secondary schools could become even greater.

College Attendance Among People of Color

Among the more than 25 million 18–24-year-olds in 1990 nationally, there were some 3.5 million African Americans. That year, 2,710,000 (77%) of this total group of African American 18–24-year-olds completed or had completed high school and 894,000, or 33% of high school graduates attended a 2- or 4-year college. If we look at the full cohort of graduates that year, we see that less than half as many Hispanics (29%) of the same age range enrolled in college. However, more than seven times as many Whites (over 39%) of the same age enrolled in college. Thus begins the road to racial and ethnic disparity between America's teachers and students.[18] In 1990, there were a total of 2,706,000 students of color enrolled in all institutions of higher education. They constituted 19.5% of the total postsecondary enrollment, and that percentage rose only to 24.3 in 1997.[19]

Enrollments in Schools, Colleges, and Departments of Education

If we look one year later (1991), allowing students to settle into their majors, we see that of the 543,382 students enrolled in undergraduate, post-baccalaureate, and doctoral programs in schools, colleges, and departments of education in America, 460,377 (84.7%) were White, while 65,041 (11.9%) were students of color.[20] The disparity continues to widen and widens further still when we look specifically at undergraduate enrollments in schools, colleges, and departments of education. We narrow our focus to this group because they no doubt could provide a major source of newly hired teachers of color in the future. On the undergraduate level in 1991, there were 39,991 students of color enrolled, 11.5% of the total,[21] a percentage that rose to only 19.5% in 1995.

In 1991, 8,707,000 students were enrolled in 4-year institutions. Of these, 1,573,000, or 18%, were students of color. But of these million and a half students of color, only 39,991, a mere 2.5%, were enrolled in schools, colleges, and departments of education (SCDEs). Only 4.4% of the 6,744,000 White students enrolled in 4-year institutions were enrolled in SCDEs, but that percentage represented almost 300,000 White students. The numbers for Hispanic, Asian/Pacific Islander, and Native American students are even smaller. So the outcome, as suggested below, will be a very limited pool of graduates of color from education programs.

Education Degrees Conferred upon People of Color

In the 1993–94 academic year, the 106,954 bachelor of education degrees conferred were distributed racially and ethnically as noted in Table 2.2.

Education graduates of color, the vast majority of whom (76.5%) are women, number only 11,472, and they make up only 10.7% of the earners of B.A. degrees in education. Although this number represents a slight increase over the 10,307 education graduates of color in the previous year,[22] one wonders just how much of a gain they possibly can represent in the movement toward racial and ethnic parity between students and classroom teachers. In the latest figures available for 1997, just over 14,000 of the more than 105,000 undergraduate degrees in education were conferred upon people of color.[23]

New Entrants of Color into the Teaching Force

What gains can be made in the diversity of the teaching force, even when we factor in the 12,919 people of color who earned master's degrees in education in 1993–94 or the approximately 15,000 who did so in 1997? As Darling-Hammond, Dilworth, and Bullmaster indicates, "In 1985, about 74 percent of the total number of those qualified to teach applied for teaching jobs, and just under 50 percent taught full-time. However, only 38 percent of the newly certified candidates of color entered teaching full time."[24] If we apply this rate of 38% to our 1993–94 cohort of 11,472 education graduates of color, the yield for the teaching corps would be only around 4,300 "newly minted" teachers of color nationally.

New teachers of color represent a small portion of the total pool of entering teachers. In 1993–94, there were 2,561,294 public elementary and second-

Table 2.2. Bachelor's Degrees in Education by Race and Gender, 1993–94.

	Male		Female	
	Number	Percent of Total	Number	Percent of Total
White	21,549	20.0	73,933	68.7
African American	1,477	1.3	4,839	4.4
Hispanic	746	*	2,549	2.3
Asian/Pacific Islander	270	*	852	0.7
Native American	199	*	540	*

Note: * indicates less than 0.1%.
Source: National Center for Education Statistics. (1995). *Digest of education statistics,* Table 260, p. 287.

ary school teachers.[25] Of these, 11.8% were newly hired, but 7.5% were newly hired and experienced,[26] so that the crop of first-time newly hired teachers constituted 4.3% of the total teaching force, or around 110,000 people. The 4,300 people of color with newly conferred B.A.s in education thus seem to form a rather small trickle into the total pool of 110,000 new teachers nationally.

Teacher Mobility Statistics

The statistics on new entrants become even more significant when viewed in the context of teacher mobility statistics. Between the years 1990–91 and 1991–92, 6.1% of African American and 4.4% of Hispanic public school teachers left teaching. Further, 8.3% of African American and 6.0% of Hispanic public school teachers changed schools.[27] Thus, it seems apparent that little gain currently is being made in diversifying the American teaching force. In fact, the percentage of teachers of color in American elementary and secondary schools actually decreased from 13.2% in 1991 to 9.3% in 1996. Thus, approximately one out of ten public school teachers is a person of color.[28]

Regarding mobility of teachers at private schools, 15.4% of "minority" teachers left teaching between 1990–91 and 1991–92, and 5.3% of "minority" teachers at private schools changed to teaching jobs at other schools.[29] However, these figures do not specifically reflect teacher mobility at NAIS schools.

Potential Pool of Uncertified Teachers for Independent Schools

Among the positive signs for public and independent schools seeking to become more diverse is the fact that, even though the number of B.A.s in education earned by people of color has remained rather low at 9,973, or 6%, the total number of B.A. degrees earned by people of color in all fields has risen rather steadily between 1977 and 1992 to 164,983.[30] Thus, the pool of potential independent school teachers of color in 1992 had perhaps grown, if we consider that many of these graduates could have applied for independent school teaching jobs without certification. We may find a source of optimism in the fact that in 1992, over 55,000 students of color (33.5%) earned B.A.s in the humanities and social/behavioral sciences, and another 38,311 (23%) earned B.A.s in health sciences. In 1996–97, just over 47,000 students of color earned B.A. degrees in the humanities, social sciences, and languages and literature, while just under 47,000 earned business degrees.[31]

Pearl Rock Kane conducted a survey of 1,218 seniors in the 1989 graduating classes of Columbia College and Barnard College, asking whether they "would consider taking a teaching job in a public elementary or secondary school if one were offered for the September following graduation."[32] Two out of every three respondents said they would. She concluded, "If the Columbia/Barnard sample of students is at all representative," there might be a potential pool of 36% of all liberal arts graduates who might be willing to teach, a national pool of some 115,000 at the time the study was done. While most students stated that they would be willing to teach for only a few years, "in urban school districts, 50 percent of the beginning teachers leave within five years," and "in all U.S. school districts 50 percent of the beginning teachers leave within six years."[33] The findings of Kane's study are especially interesting for independent schools because students in the study cited the following as among their three main discouragements from teaching in public schools: first, an unwillingness to undergo the time and expense of certification; second, low salaries; and finally, the fact that no one had recruited them. More than a third of the Black students who were surveyed said that they would be influenced by on-campus recruitment. Thus, there may be ways of increasing the pool of teachers of color that have not yet been fully utilized. And yet, there are a number of factors that have prevented people of color from selecting teaching as a career.

WHY PEOPLE OF COLOR ARE NOT CHOOSING TEACHING

Most scholars who have carefully studied the matter agree that three central factors have limited the participation of teachers of color in the profession of teaching: the low socioeconomic status and poor education of children of color; the imposition of competency tests during the reform surge of the 1980s; and the exodus of people of color to more lucrative, higher-status professions in the wake of the Civil Rights Movement and the advent of affirmative action and increased professional opportunities.

Low SES/Lack of Quality Education

We have already examined the persistently low rate at which young people of color are completing high school, entering college, and completing degree studies, even within 6 years of entering college. A few researchers have reviewed the record of inequality of educational opportunity and achievement between children of color (specifically African Americans) and Euro-American children. As often has been demonstrated, African Americans and Latinos are more likely to be enrolled in special education programs or placed into general education and vocational tracks, while Euro-American students more often are placed in gifted programs. Euro-American students also take more years of coursework in math, social studies, and physical science.[34]

Researcher Martin Haberman asks pointedly how we can expect Blacks and Hispanics who have grown up predominantly in urban school systems to consider the profession of teaching when, "among their 50 teachers and countless substitutes," they have seen "lifers" and "burnouts on the one hand," and, on the other, "caring and effective teachers demonstrating feelings of powerlessness."[35] With their own frequently negative experiences in urban schools, undergraduates of color may come to view the teaching profession as embodying a negative daily experience. Almost half of the 140 respondents in June Gordon's study said that young people of color avoided the teaching profession because of their perception that students lack discipline and teachers are not respected.[36]

Linda Darling-Hammond recalls how, during the 1980s, "the pool of eligible entrants to teaching was limited by several kinds of competency tests initiated by 46 states for admission into teacher education programs, exit from programs, and/or for certification."[37] Many have illustrated that such tests clearly eliminated "minority" test takers at a much higher rate than they eliminated White test takers.[38] Cole and Irvine have argued for the elimination of competency tests on the basis that they do not measure real competency in teaching and are culturally biased.[39] Some have argued for multiple forms of assessment based on the fact that teaching is not a one-dimensional science.[40] Researchers Johnson and Prom-Jackson surveyed 813 graduates of the A Better Chance (ABC) program that placed talented minority students in independent schools. They tried to determine qualities, beyond measurable intellectual competencies, that make one an effective and truly memorable teacher. They found that "while talented students are strongly influenced toward academic growth and development during their school years, the way in which this happens, according to the perceptions of respondents, is through the interpersonal skills and affective characteristics of good teachers."[41] Thus, strong arguments were advanced against the belief that one-dimensional measures of intellect that focus heavily on content mastery are sufficient to determine teacher competency, even when the subjects being considered are excellence-driven independent school teachers. Gifford argues that

> If there is indeed a national commitment to quality education for all, as a part of our dedication to the principles of equality, then suggestions to change the [testing] requirements to fit the present median performance of minority teachers will be ignored. . . . To put forth the argument that low-income minority youngsters . . . should be taught by less than the best teachers is to stand the idea of justice on its head.[42]

After the flurry of articles written about competency testing in the 1980s, a pronounced quietness about the issue set in during the 1990s. When we asked Deborah J. Carter of the American Council on Education about this, she confirmed that the quality agenda had gained such a level of acceptance that leaders in higher education had "rolled up their sleeves and gotten to work on better supporting and preparing students of color."[43]

Attraction to Other Professions

On the relevance of financial incentives in attracting people of color into teaching, Dilworth has stated

> Although teacher salaries have improved . . . there is a general perception of a low cost-benefit ratio for the field. Since Blacks and other minorities attend college with greater loan burdens than others, and minority women carry greater responsibility for household income than their majority peers, the decision to enter teaching is often a sacrifice.[44]

Several studies have confirmed Dilworth's point. Gordon found that of the 140 teachers of color she interviewed in Cincinnati, Ohio; Seattle, Washington; and Long Beach, California, "one half of all informants stated low pay as the main reason students of color were not entering teaching."[45]

Opening of Other, Higher-Prestige Professions

Salary as a disincentive for people of color to go into teaching is closely coupled with the disincentive of the lack of status, respect, and prestige that is associated with teaching in many people's minds. In her history of Blacks in the teaching profession, Perkins chronicles the way in which African Americans, after years of being revered as community mentors because they persisted in teaching under horrible conditions, lost their jobs in disproportionate numbers with the *Brown* decision and the start of school integration. What ensued, Perkins contends, was an African American exodus to other professions newly opened in the wake of the Civil Rights Movement, professions that pulled capable, strong African Americans, who were potential role models and community leaders, away from their home communities.[46] As King suggests, "Careers in law, medicine, other health professions, computer science and engineering have become more popular and accessible to individuals of color."[47] She further affirms that for the past quarter of a century, over 80% of all teachers have been first-generation college graduates."[48] As other careers have opened up to people of color, and as their parents have become college graduates themselves in increasing numbers, they have avoided what King refers to as the traditional "stepping-stone" of teaching.[49]

Asian/Pacific Islander Americans also seem to avoid what they perceive as the lower status of teaching, even though in many Asian cultures teachers are revered. Asian parents play a particularly strong role in influencing their children's choice of college or course of study. According to Chinn and Wong (1992), "The fields of study selected are characteristically those with high extrinsic rewards coupled with high prestige, such as medicine, dentistry, . . . engineering, . . . accounting, and computer science." Thus, the authors conclude, "To become a teacher, Asian males and females may have to consciously disappoint their parents."[50]

Just how the issues of compensation, status, and image of the profession will interact to attract teachers of color to public or independent schools now and in the years ahead is a complex issue.

LESSONS FROM PUBLIC-SECTOR RECRUITING OF TEACHERS OF COLOR

Public-Sector Recruitment Efforts

If America hopes to create a more diverse and representative teaching force, the most obvious step that must be taken, scholars agree, is the immediate improvement of K–12 education for all children, but most urgently for children of color in poor urban and rural districts.[51]

Essentially, three kinds of recruitment initiatives were employed throughout the 1980s and 1990s, with varying and often unquantifiable measures of success: precollege recruitment programs focused on middle and high school students; university level (including community college) recruitment and retention programs; and mid-career or alternate route programs.[52]

PreCollege Recruitment Programs

The success of precollege programs and initiatives that have been developed to recruit young people of color into teaching have been catalogued and analyzed in some detail by the Massachusetts organization, Recruiting New Teachers, in its 1993 study, "Teaching's Next Generation: A National Study of Pre-Collegiate Teacher Recruitment." One type of program, not at all widely replicated, is the pre-professional magnet school or teacher academy, in which a whole school or part of a school is focused not only on traditional content but on teaching itself. These schools normally include such elements as teacher mentors, student tutoring programs within school or at other schools with younger children, shadowing experiences, and summer activities, often on a college campus. In some cases loan forgiveness programs and scholarships have been capstones to such programs.[53] Short of such school-wide initiatives, schools have offered individual courses, summer programs and workshops, clubs, and assembly programs on teaching as a career.

Postsecondary Recruitment Efforts

At the university level, many programs from the late 1980s onward began focusing on community college students, a large percentage of whom are students of color. Key ingredients to programs that seek to recruit community college students into education majors are a smooth transfer process with clear guidance; designated financial aid as at Florida International University; and academic support and guidance at both the community college and university level. Gonzalez studied three grant-funded preservice programs at six institutions to determine the elements that minority preservice teachers found most important.[54] Students most frequently cited: "the human dimension"; caring mentors; low bureaucracy/close contact; peer recruitment; early and intense experience in schools; bridging experiences to ease transition to college; learning to learn (developing skills); structured and systematic monitoring of progress; and clearly maintained academic standards.

Recruitment by "Headhunters"

A more recent method for recruiting teachers of color that is being used by public school districts and consortia of districts, and which may offer clues for independent schools, is the use of what Richardson termed "talent scouts," district human resources or personnel officers whose sole function (in some cases) is to travel to colleges and job fairs seeking to lure candidates to their districts. For instance, Broward County, Florida, the eighth largest district in the nation, among whose 200,000 students 50% are "minority," has employed six full-time recruiters. In 10 years, the percentage of minority teachers has risen from 5 to 32. Similarly, recruiters from Prince George's County, Maryland, 70% of whose students are Black, travel annually in a motor home to a number of historically Black colleges; of the county's 600 new hires last year, 47% were Black.[55] Perhaps the lesson for independent schools here is that aggressive recruitment yields results. These figures also hearken back to the responses in Kane's study of Columbia and Barnard graduates, among whom graduates of color reported that they would be positively influenced by on-campus recruitment.

TEACHER INDUCTION AND RETENTION PRACTICES

A final area where programs developed in the public sector may shed important light on the ways independent schools seek to diversify faculties is the induction and retention practices being employed in some areas. Traditionally, independent schools, with their emphasis on autonomy, have been sink or swim operations, in which new teachers have been largely left to their own resources, with occasional help from department chairs or older colleagues. The pressure is heightened by the fact that "consumerist" parents at schools with a college preparatory focus may be waiting in the wings to swarm all over a teacher who is "ineffective." A young teacher of color entering such a scenario in a world that may be culturally shocking to begin with easily can feel alienated.

A. L. Smith describes successful induction/mentoring programs, such as the Retired Teacher Mentor Program run jointly by the New York City Board of Education, the CUNY Center for Advanced Study in Education, and Barnard College, in which retired teachers work in the classroom alongside new teachers in schools with high attrition and dropout rates. An even more comprehensive program described by Smith is the Hunter College and District Four (East Harlem) collaborative, Training Tomorrow's Teachers, which works with first-year minority teachers. Both mentors and novices are granted release time to visit each other's classes. Meanwhile, two graduate courses are offered on-site, tuition-free, by Hunter College faculty, who aid mentors in counseling students.[56]

Going even a step further to aid induction of new teachers of color, Prince George's County, Maryland, offers not only after-school and weekend workshops and a buddy system for new teachers of color, but also the Beginning Teacher Assistance Program, which offers various incentives to new teachers, such as a free month's apartment rent, waiver of security deposits, furniture discounts, and discounts on car loans.[57] Independent schools, especially those associated with the now defunct Independent School Opportunity Program funded by Dewitt Wallace/Reader's Digest, have made strides in offering mentor programs for all new teachers. In fact, Lawrenceville School developed a manual for mentoring at independent schools that has been distributed at conferences and workshops. However, no such programs to ease the transition to a new living environment for first-year teachers of color at independent day schools have yet been written or studied.

HISTORY OF FACULTY DIVERSITY
AT INDEPENDENT SCHOOLS

When one considers the number of local, state, and national programs for the recruitment of teachers of color (including the many that have come and gone), one feels that the issue has truly taken on national significance. The sense of urgency about the issue no doubt is fueled by the fact that schools are just not succeeding in reaching and preparing children of color. We may question the extent to which independent schools have participated and will participate in this national movement toward greater diversity in the teaching force. A sketch of the history of diversity in independent schools, brief and impressionistic as it no doubt will prove to be, should help.

Arthur Powell, in his recent study of independent schools, says the following:

> Veteran teachers who had attended prep schools in the 1950's could recall decades later the tiny number of racial and religious minorities who were their schoolmates. Before the 1960's, Jews were far more problematic than Blacks; many more Jews wanted to attend, could afford to pay, and easily met admissions criteria. . . . Unlike Blacks, who after 1963 became the most sought-after . . . group in the history of American education, Jews were never recruited by prep schools at all. . . . Nearly five percent of Andover students were Jews in the 1940's. The Head wanted that number reduced, lest it frighten away his mainly Protestant constituency.[58]

We quote at length because Powell's statement makes a number of crucial points. First it tells us that independent schools, if we take Andover as something of a prototype, have had a long-standing consciousness of their markets, and the distinctive features that will either draw or repel those markets. As such they have been quite image-conscious throughout their histories. Powell, in fact, goes on to say that "although it was initially a practical economic and public relations strategy, many private schools claimed by the end of the 1960's to value diversity as a positive good."[59] The initial statement by Powell above also tells us something more about the history of diversity at independent schools. Although the topic seems to be one of the most guarded in American education, references in various sources indicate that the 1960s marked the beginning of conscious efforts to diversify by mainstream independent prep schools (from which, of course, we exclude segregation academies).

In fact, Powell reports, "only about twenty independent schools enrolled any Black students by 1948, and as late as 1960 only about one-third had ever enrolled a Black student."[60] To get an idea of the degree of diversity among students that developed during the 1960s in independent schools, we turn to the ambitious study of private and independent schools done by Otto Kraushaar in 1972.

KRAUSHAAR'S STUDY

Kraushaar reports that of 119 schools in his sample, 71 elementary and secondary schools (or 59.7%) responded that they did have Black students during the 1968–69 school year. Among strictly secondary schools, reported by region, the responses to questions about Black enrollment and ethnic enrollment fell into the pattern depicted in Table 2.3.

Thus, out of 31,179 students at the 64 schools responding that they did have some African American enrollment, 883, or 2.8%, were African American. A total of 1,213 students, or 3.9% constituted the total racial/ethnic enrollment (includes "Black American, American Indian, Mexican American, Puerto Rican American, Oriental American") at the 104 schools sampled, which perhaps gives us a fairly accurate picture of the diversity at NAIS schools at the time. Kraushaar further tells us that in the NAIS "Minority Group Survey" for 1969–70, out of 770 member schools, 752 responded, and 730 stated they had an open enrollment policy, although of these, 99 had never enrolled a Black student. The 595 member schools with Black students admitted 7,617 Black students. It is significant and hopeful that the number is more than twice the number admitted in 1966–67.[61]

Kraushaar tells us nothing about the degree of diversity among NAIS faculties at the time, perhaps because there was virtually no diversity. At the time of Kraushaar's study, in the northeast, roughly 10% of parents and 10% of trustees are opposed to integrating the faculty. In the south, roughly 70% of parents and 70% of trustees are opposed. And in midwest and far west schools, almost 25% of board members and 40% of parents are opposed to faculty integration.

THE BEGINNINGS OF DIVERSITY AT NAIS SCHOOLS

The year 1963, which is pointed to by many scholars as a turning point in independent school diversity, witnessed the beginnings of concerted efforts on behalf of independent schools to recruit "Negro" students. In December of that year NAIS published a pamphlet by David Mallery called "Negro Stu-

Table 2.3. Students Diversity in Selected Independent Schools, 1968–69.

Region	Number Responding "Yes" (Total: 64 out of 104)	Percentage of Black Enrollment	Percentage of Students of Color Enrollment	Percentage Responding "Yes"
Northeast	32 out of 41	3.5	4.6	78
South	4 out of 26	0.3	1.5	15
Midwest and Far West	28 out of 37	3.7	4.7	76

Source: Kraushaar, O. F. (1972). *American non-public schools*, Table 7, pp. 238–239.

dents in Independent Schools," which was, in effect, a recruitment guide, a moral guide to the reasons for accepting Negro students, a primer on how to deal with issues of campus integration, and a guide for admissions directors, who were told to be willing to "gamble" on talented but perhaps under-prepared applicants.[62] Reference frequently is made to the National Scholar-ship Service and Fund for Negro Students (NSSFNS), which had worked with college-bound students primarily on placement and scholarship, but then moved into independent school placement. NSSFNS was in many ways the predecessor to the programs that followed, like ABC, which, "in its first de-cade served almost 4,000 students and spent nearly 40 million dollars."[63] Through the efforts of such collaborative programs as Project Broad Jump, Horizons-Upward Bound, and ABC, "the number of integrated prep schools jumped from 33 percent in 1960 to 84 percent in 1969. Black enrollment tripled to 4.3 percent in the decade ending in 1975 and approached 11,000 students."[64] The key ingredients to such programs were committed, collabo-rative efforts and sufficient funding.

The history of diversity at southern independent schools is a history unto itself. In the 100 schools belonging to the Mid-South Association of Indepen-dent Schools (MAIS), Z. Vance Wilson reports, there were 357 Black students in 1978–79. The following year there were 760 students. "That number was 1.5 percent of the total population of 51,085 students."[65] Wilson also informs us that in the 100 MAIS schools

> Black teacher employment in 1979–80 was 15 persons. By school year 1982–83 the number was 27. During that period of time it is estimated there were 460 teacher vacancies. . . . As has been the experience of the National Associa-tion of Independent Schools, students clearly led the way in integration.[66]

Wilson goes on to chronicle the gradual increase in diversity of students and teachers in MAIS schools through the courageous and persistent efforts of school heads and through the provisions of a Lyndhurst Foundation grant for minority scholarships and teacher recruitment. By 1980–81, "total minor-ity enrollment increased from 3.4 percent to 4.0 percent, 2,026 students."[67] At the time, NAIS total minority enrollment was 7%. However, by 1983, 65% of the MAIS schools still did not have one minority teacher or administrator.

STUDENT DIVERSITY AT NAIS SCHOOLS OVER TIME

If we have dwelled on the growth of student diversity, it is because we be-lieve Wilson is right in stating that students have led the way and are leading the way in the diversification of NAIS schools. So we ask at this point, what paths have student and faculty diversity taken at independent schools? The National Association of Independent Schools has been gathering and publishing statistics on student diversity, enrollment, financial aid, salaries, and other features of member schools since 1981–82.

We may start with bits from various sources to determine that in 1968–69, total minority enrollment was perhaps 3.8%, according to Kraushaar's representative sample of over 31,000 students in 64 schools. It grew to 7% in 1980–81, according to Wilson's statements above, and climbed further to 9.1% in 1981–82. From that point onward, the percentage of students of color grew slowly but steadily until 1996–97, with slight dips in 1994 and 1997, which may be due in part to the smaller number of schools reporting in those years.

Starting from Powell's assertion that Black enrollment was 4.3% in 1975, we see a slight dip in African American students enrolled to 4.2% in 1982, but from there, the percentage grows almost imperceptibly to 5% in 1989. As of 2002, the percentage of African American students enrolled has never reached higher than 5.8%.[68] Hispanic students since 1982 essentially have hovered between 2 and 3% of total student population. Native American students have remained a very small part of the student population. Asian/Pacific Islander Americans, on the other hand, have grown the most significantly as a percentage of total students enrolled, starting as a smaller percentage of total students than African Americans in 1982, matching them in 1987, and surpassing them more and more significantly from 1990 onward. This may be largely a function of the income status of Asian Americans, cited earlier in this chapter. However, as we discovered in an exploratory visit with Lesley Sedehi and Martha Lucia Galindo in the statistics office at NAIS, the numbers and percentages of Asian students include Hawaii, a fact that may skew results. In our 1997 analysis of the NAIS database, when we excluded Hawaii from the figures, as perhaps we should have since Asian/Pacific Islander students can't really be considered diverse or "minority" in Hawaii. Then, the number of Asian students in NAIS schools dropped from 16,538 to 5,372, a decrease of over 11,000 students in NAIS schools. This changed the percentage of Asian/Pacific Islander students in NAIS schools from 8.2 to 5.7.

Furthermore, the U.S. Territories, which included Puerto Rico, accounted for over 1,000 Hispanic students. When we discounted these students, there were 2.6% Hispanic students in NAIS schools rather than 2.8%. This change, taken together with the adjustments for Asian/Pacific Islander students above, altered the total percentage of students of color in 1995–96 in NAIS schools from 16.7 to 14.2 and raised questions about what we can really conclude from such broad annual statistics. What did it really mean for the diversity of independent schools that there were approximately 22,000 African American students enrolled in 1997, when we consider that they were dispersed among a sea of some 416,000 students in NAIS schools? And how were they dispersed?

How much of an impact could their presence have had at any given school or in any particular region? In 1999, how visible were the 23,630 African American students who attended NAIS schools among the total of 421,306 students?

FACULTY DIVERSITY AT NAIS SCHOOLS OVER TIME

> The need for and importance of having minority teachers on independent school campuses is the same today as it was in 1970, when NAIS launched its special five-year minority recruitment project. Prospects for future success may be a bit brighter because we now know much, much more about the factors and conditions that make it possible for independent schools to attract and retain minority teachers.[69]

What is striking about this statement is not just that it was written in 1978 but that it begins an article on how to recruit "minority" teachers that easily could have been published as the current wisdom only a month ago. After talking about changing career paths and aspirations of "minority people," Dandridge offers suggestions on how to recruit: getting in touch with minority graduates; networking with minority parents; networking with college placement offices; developing teacher apprentice programs; and networking with other schools to share knowledge of minority candidates. If these ideas sound familiar, it may be because many of them were touched upon in the section on recruitment efforts earlier in this chapter and because they are still being talked about constantly at conferences and workshops on diversity at independent schools.

Teachers of color in independent schools grew from 4.3% of the total teaching force in 1986–87 to 7% in 1996–97, a "79.5 percent increase."[70] These numbers mean there were roughly 3,000 teachers of color out of approximately 45,000. Even if they were evenly distributed across the 953 member schools in 1996, which was not the case, we would have found only perhaps two or three teachers of color at any given NAIS school. At these same schools, in 1996, students of color and Euro-American students would have seen among the clerical staff, maintenance workers, kitchen staff, and security crew, 20% people of color. In schools of the southeast and New England regions, only 4.5% and 5.8% of teachers, respectively, were people of color. Ironically, for every school that through its enlightened and earnest efforts has developed a truly diverse faculty, there are several other schools with no teachers of color. In the most recent NAIS Statistics (1999), there is no breakdown of teachers by ethnicity, as traditionally has been the case. The statistics suggest that 7.3% of NAIS teachers, 2,770 out of some 38,000, were people of color, at least among an indeterminate number of "core sample members."[71]

My Chance Encounter with Independent Schools

Dennis Bisgaard
Shady Hill School, MA

I vividly remember my chance encounter with the independent school world, a world I knew absolutely nothing about but that has since become a signifi-cant part of my life. I stumbled upon independent schools on a late Saturday afternoon in April 1989. After several hours of intense pick-up basketball games at McGonigle Hall at Temple University, I sat soaking in the bathtub, reading a book, when the phone rang. As a foreign graduate student on a year-long fellowship, I seldom received phone calls. Ironically, my long-instilled child-hood caution about water, electricity, and the danger of electrocution was the first thought that entered my mind. Nonetheless, I decided to take the risk and picked up the phone. If I hadn't on that very afternoon, when I felt a special surge of energy and a greater adventurousness than usual, I would have left the States a few months later to resume my life in Denmark.

On the other end of the phone, Dr. Beards's cheery voice greeted me, as it had on other occasions when he had called to check in with me. Dr. Beards, a department chair at Temple, was my mentor and the local contact from the Thanks to Scandinavia Foundation, which the year before had selected me as its first "Fellow" to study African and African American literature and culture. I had been chosen, in part I believe, because from an early age as part of my own identity formation process, I had read everything I could get my hands on and taken every course pertaining to the African American experience. As you can imagine, the course offering on that particular subject was sparse at a univer-sity in Denmark. However, for a Danish citizen I was well versed and had chosen to write my dissertation on Toni Morrison before she reached her status as a literary genius. And, for all I know, I may be the only Dane who has considered *The Autobiography of Malcolm X* his personal Bible at one point in his life.

As we spoke, Dr. Beards asked me, "So what are you going to do once you leave the States—what is life after Temple going to look like?" Without thinking long, I blurted out what had been embedded in my mind for a while: "If I could, I would love to stay in the States longer, but I know that . . . "

Although life as a foreigner had been quite isolating and challenging as I tried to understand and get my mind around "America," I felt I was just beginning to know this place that had attracted me for so long. Living most of my life in Europe, I liked my new surroundings and the exposure to people of color in particular. For once in my life, I was not the only one.

In his wonderful "matter of fact" and "anything is possible approach," Dr. Beards told me that he would call a friend who was the English department chair at a private school in Baltimore. The conversation soon ended, and, although I sensed a brief glimmer of hope, I didn't think much about the exchange until one day when, to my great surprise, Peter Bailey called me to set up an interview. The day was arranged. I took the train to Baltimore and entered the private school world and single-sex education with the naiveté of a blissfully ignorant newcomer who knows too little to be overly impressed or nervous about the event. In fact, I rather enjoyed the day as I was showered with attention, and the interview itself was a welcome break from my lonely foreign experience. Often while I was at Temple, the dichotomy of being the "Scandinavian Scholar" with access to a rich world of academia, and of feeling at an utter loss trying to comprehend my new and confusing environment, was overwhelming and profound. In my mind, the girls' school, in contrast, felt like familiar ground and manageable. More important, the school seemed like a welcoming community where I could belong. I gladly accepted the year-long appointment at minimum pay as an intern, a position that had become available because a teacher had been granted a leave of absence on short notice. To be honest, I considered my "job" more like another chance to extend my American experience than a first building stone to launching my career within independent schools.

I was in my mid-twenties; I had taught high school English and PE in Denmark; I had played and coached sports competitively for a long time; and, maybe most significant, I came with what many consider a very interesting, diverse background. I am a person of color, biracial, a transracial adoptee, and an immigrant who speaks several languages; and I had already lived in Germany, Denmark, and Canada before coming to the United States. The intertwined roots of my birth and adopted families originate in Germany, Trinidad, Denmark, Black America, Korea, Mexico, and Argentina. Later, I added to my "profile" by marrying an African American woman and becoming a father to our bi (or is it tri?) racial son. Thus, "diversity" as it seems to pertain to "people of color" has always been part of my life, long before these terms or "multiculturalism" entered my vocabulary or my consciousness. Ironically, I did not attach much meaning to my "diversity status" since it had been a fact of life since the day I was born. I simply wanted to take in "America" a little longer, and teaching at a school allowed me to do so. That it was a private school, in my mind, simply meant that I was allowed to work without any special certification.

Thinking back to my rookie year, I realize that my first American teaching job was ideal. I lived inexpensively in the only faculty apartment on cam-

pus, people treated me well, and I taught two sections of eighth-grade English with only one preparation. In addition, I found myself in familiar terri-
tory during PE classes, and I was encouraged to develop a volleyball program
and become the varsity coach for the upper school team. Had I had a full
English teaching load that first year and not been placed in situations that
genuinely validated my strengths and enabled me to encounter successes along
the way, my experience might have been quite different. Although I can only
guess, in retrospect, I do believe that being a foreigner and the only male of
color on a faculty that consisted mostly of women helped me gain the special
kind of attention that other faculty of color may have received to a lesser
extent.

Although I had prior teaching experience, Danish and American schools
are worlds apart. My first eighth-grade girls, however, quickly taught me a
great deal about teaching and independent school culture as they tested,
stretched, humored, and ultimately worked with and for me. While I did not
fully realize it at the time, my support system was deep and far-reaching. Katie
Dallam, a seasoned fellow eighth-grade English teacher, took me under her
wing from day one as she taught me many tricks of the trade without ever
overcrowding me or becoming patronizing. Magically, quizzes, assignment
sheets, tests, and "just FYI" notes always seemed to find their way to my
mailbox, and our many casual chats contained an abundance of "golden nuggets" about teaching, classroom management, and assessment. The middle
school director and the school head were always there to answer any question I might have, even the ones I did not articulate because I simply did not
know enough to ask them. Before my first meeting with parents, the school
head pulled me aside to role play a potential worst-case scenario: how to respond to the question parents might ask about the qualifications or abilities
of a relatively young Dane of color with a slight accent teaching their daughters English. No parent ever voiced the concern; however, had I been asked
the question, I would have known what and how to answer. I do believe that
a number of faculty of color at times find themselves blindsided in similar
situations that occur without this kind of frank and raw input. Over the years,
I have witnessed too many individuals tiptoe around faculty of color out of
fear of giving the wrong impression. Unfortunately, in the process, inexperienced faculty of color, in particular, are not provided with adequate input
about potentially challenging experiences, or about shortcomings that need
to be addressed.

I can laugh at my own early rookie mistakes now, but at the time I often
felt like I had entered the deepest circle of Dante's *Inferno* with no means to
escape. Despite my 6'3" frame, graduate degrees in English and PE, a successful
career as an athlete, and some prior teaching experience, my class of eighth-
grade girls could decide my "fate" on any given day as I entered their "do-

main." Yet, even on the worst of days, Peter, Cornelia, and Katie were in my corner to patch me up, boost my bruised ego, and help me make sense of it all. Their genuine interest in seeing me succeed and grow as a teacher made a world of difference, and in that light it was much easier to receive feedback about areas in which I clearly still had some growing to do. Furthermore, even as a young and inexperienced teacher, I always felt welcome in the headmistress' office; she would always take the time to listen, chat, and answer any question that I might have.

Circumstances in faculty attrition and my solid first year enabled me to become a full-time faculty member. In subsequent years, even with a full English load and coaching three seasons, I was able to focus on becoming a better teacher. I taught every grade from eighth through senior electives, and I learned more and more about the school culture and subcultures.

Although I was the only biracial African American, this school had the most diverse faculty and student body I have experienced (to this day), and thus I found myself in the luxurious and uncommon situation within independent schools of engaging in frequent conversations with students, faculty, and staff of color. Most faculty of color were in the lower school or in art and music, whereas the two upper school teachers of color were both of international background. Early on when I was asked to consider becoming the faculty advisor to the Black Awareness Club, I simply said yes. Yet, in retrospect I often have wondered what I, having spent most of my life in Germany and Denmark, could offer the group. I certainly had experienced plenty of personal racism and bias. I had read a lot, and I clearly was a person of color. But I was also a male with a very different background and life experience from those of my students. Did my life experience and the pigmentation of my skin make me a more appropriate candidate for the job than a White individual who had lived his or her entire life in America? My intuition told me no, but I took on the responsibility and learned much in the process about the intricate entanglement of race relations in America. My eyes were opened wide to new worlds as I was allowed to enter the often quite different reality and experience of both students and faculty of color. I still remember April Johnson, a junior at the time, who one day, after a particularly interesting and thoughtful discussion on *A Passage to India*, came up to me at the end of class. "Mr. Bisgaard, some folks don't see you as Black, but I know that you are Black on the inside."

Obviously, I was somewhat surprised by her comment, but it made me realize that she needed to tell me that I somehow had been able to convey to her that I genuinely cared, supported, and intuitively understood her experience also. I have felt connected to all of my students, but over the years I have come to realize that my mere presence is significant to students of color in particular. The invisible ties that bind people of color together within independent schools are powerful, and I often marvel at what at times seems like an entirely different reality. Diversity within independent schools, and society at large for that matter, is so hard to get at because people simply do not see, experience, or feel what others do, or diversity somehow pertains only to race and ethnicity. Although "multiple realities" is a buzz word these days, I am not sure that we are even close to understanding the multiple realities of all of our students, families, and faculty. While my identity, as everyone else's, is made up of a mosaic of intricate and interconnected pieces that are shaped according to past experiences, present conditions, and future aspirations, being a male of color often has been the one component that has been highlighted.

I gradually became the diversity voice of my first school and found myself organizing "multicultural" events and leading discussions involving a number of constituencies on race, ethnicity, gender, and sexual identity. I think I did a decent job, but like most diversity coordinators in independent schools, I had no official training or expertise, nor did I have a budget, any assistance, or any power to effect change. And, I taught a full load of classes and coached. My own experience was positive. I learned a lot, and I had plenty of energy. However, I have seen many young, inexperienced people of color placed in no-win situations as institutional diversity experts. How does one person, an inexperienced teacher no less, begin to tackle the issues of institutional climate and change? Ironically, by the time the most astute diversity coordinators see the larger picture or understand the multiple layers of an institution, they are often burned out or unwilling to shoulder the burden of being the diversity agent for change. And, if they are not completely drained, they often conclude that a diversity position is a dead-end job that can be a roadblock if one has ambitions to climb the administrative ladder. In my second job, after 3 years, I quite deliberately began working my way out of my administrative diversity position because I refused to be slotted in the diversity box.

As a new teacher, and ever since, I have attended annual NAIS People of Color Conferences, the significance of which I wish people within independent schools at large could fully comprehend and therefore support. For many educators of color, the annual gathering is so much more than a professional conference. When one works in predominantly mainstream schools, there is something profoundly powerful about simply being in the midst of more than a thousand educators of color from across the country. Many faculty of color return from the conference with a renewed sense of purpose and self, and some argue that they simply would not survive in their schools without this annual emotional and spiritual boost. I know of many individuals who pay their own way because their schools are unable or unwilling to support them. Although I have encountered my own share of personal traumas, "war stories," and moments of disrespect, I often count myself fortunate that I have not been exposed, from an early age, to the multilayered and multifaceted complexities of race relations in America. Thus, I may not be quite as incensed, frustrated, or angry as others. Being an insider and outsider at the same time has allowed me a certain perspective that might make my life somewhat easier than that of many other people of color within independent schools. However, the longer I have been in independent schools, the more I have gotten to know the sphere in which many faculty of color find themselves.

Some of the experiences I myself have encountered as a person of color within schools have been perplexing, bizarre, and infuriating. Even if situations do not seem grave in themselves, their combined force can affect you and keep you second-guessing. Thus, if you are hit with enough insensitive "race pellets," the impact can be immense and you sometimes do wonder whether it is worth working in such environments. How are you to respond and think about your workplace when a parent asks you whether you intend to teach English or multiculturalism in your expository writing class? How are you to respond when a fellow teacher in your first week of your new administrative job tells you, "Oh, yeah, I forgot that you were brought in at the top whereas the rest of us have to work our way up," when explaining why you have to attend a certain school function? How are you to respond when someone automatically assumes that you are the coach or music teacher rather than a teacher of English or an administrator? My own list goes on and on, and faculty of color across the country will know exactly what I am talking about because they must endure similar or sometimes more subtle experiences in their own schools everyday.

In recent years, independent schools have tended to focus on increasing their numbers of students and faculty of color, believing that "true diversity" and an appreciation of differences ultimately will follow. As long as "diversity" and "multiculturalism" are thought of as issues or constructs pertaining almost exclusively to the recruitment and retention of students and faculty of color (and for many that basically means African Americans), little progress can be made to make independent schools genuinely inclusive and accepting institutions in which all members of the community feel a sense of ownership, empowerment, and belonging. "Diversity" pertains and belongs to all of us, no matter what our background and/or our racial or ethnic makeup happens to be. Sheer numbers of people of color need to be accompanied by a school culture that engenders an authentic atmosphere of mutual respect among all members of the community. Schools need to nurture a culture of change and adaptation by weaving "newcomers," as well as their experiences, cultures, and histories, into their very fabric. However, although affective education is crucial, schools cannot go overboard and expect less than excellence. Each school needs to define precisely what "diversity" and "multiculturalism" mean within their own contexts. A genuine dialogue based on mutuality, openness, and directness needs to be encouraged and supported. When we interact with others by focusing, consciously or unconsciously, primarily on race, gender, or other social identifiers, we deprive ourselves of the mutual growth process that is involved in an exchange between equal human beings.

If I were to evaluate my own experience within independent schools for the past dozen years or so, I would say that I have encountered enough "interesting" experiences that have made life unnecessarily rough at times, but that I appreciate and understand the potentially wonderful education that can occur and is occurring and the efforts to change or adapt curricula, traditions, and cultures.

Over the years, I am glad to say that I have found allies of both genders in all shapes and colors—allies who are committed to making our schools nurturing educational environments in which all potential can be cultivated and brought to life. Currently I find myself in the position of working at a school where I would gladly send my own son. Independent schools need to become places where people of color, of different faiths, straight, gay, and lesbian, rich and poor want to send their own children because the schools are challenging educational settings, and nurturing and accepting environments. As an optimist who has witnessed change for the better, I am convinced that my own son will encounter educators of many backgrounds who will help challenge his mind and nurture his growth as a bright and caring citizen in our diverse society of tomorrow.

Gifts from the Great Spirit

Melanie Sainz
Phoenix Country Day School, AZ

Scanning through the Sunday classified section one afternoon, I found a small advertisement in the employment section of my local newspaper. I quickly responded; I mailed a copy of my resume and several slides of my personal artwork, as well as some of my students' art, to the post office box in the ad. About a week later, a school that I had never heard of before phoned me to set up the date and time for an interview. Not only had I never heard of this particular school, but I had never taught at what the assistant to the head of school described to me as an "independent day school."

To be totally honest, I really had never known the ramifications of such a place. Although my father had graduated from a small private college in the midwest, I was unaware of the significance of an independent school education. My two main concerns at the time were the availability of a teaching job in my field and my family's need for money. Art education is, unfortunately, not required in all Arizona public schools, and I had learned from my previous school that my art program easily could be put on the chopping block.

Throughout the interview process with the head of school, upper school head, middle school head, and art department chair, I emphasized the broad range of my experience: teaching at a variety of public schools throughout Arizona, providing public programs and research as the education specialist at a well-respected art museum, and facilitating grants at our local state art agency. As miracles do occur in life, I was offered the job to teach art in the middle and upper school divisions.

As I drove home from my final appointment with the school's business office, I began to consider my experience with the state art agency. In my mind, I could see the recent list of Arizona cities, ranked according to socioeconomic status. My former school was located in Komatke, a small rural community just south of Laveen on the Gila River Indian Reservation. Komatke was one of the last cities on the list. My new school would be located in the posh urban setting of Paradise Valley. It was the very first city on the list. I realized then that my daily commute would take on a whole new complexion.

I am the first American Indian faculty member hired at my school—which just celebrated its 40th anniversary. I am an enrolled member of the Hochunk

Nation of Wisconsin, formally known as the Wisconsin Winnebago. Like many others, I am a midwestern transplant in the "Valley of the Sun." I came to Arizona to attend A.S.U., and I never intended on staying here past graduation.

There is a resounding message that many American Indian students hear throughout their lives: "You're getting an education so you can come back and help your people." Well, to this day, I am reminded of this message by many back home, and I find myself struggling with the fact that I have disappointed them by remaining in Arizona for 20 years. Fortunately, a supportive, loving Latino and native Phoenician husband, as well as two terrific children, all have the uncanny ability to keep me very happy. My summer vacations regularly include as much time as possible in Wisconsin with my family, keeping me in good graces with my most of my relatives.

During my first year teaching at my current school, I questioned myself almost daily about *why* I was there. As a new faculty member teaching in two divisions, I didn't have an office space or a designated place to hang my hat, making settling in very difficult. Many students made my first year quite a memorable challenge. I saw the ways in which they criticized my clothes and hair, challenged my assignments and suggestions by seeking advice from their former art teacher, and made fun of the way that I spoke. I wondered if they had ever had a teacher who wasn't White. I would leave as soon as classes were over, and I did very little socializing with others.

At the same time, I was searching for someone who looked like me or shared my interests. I'm a visual and auditory learner, so I spent a lot of time observing people's body language and listening to conversations at the lunch table or in the teachers' lounge. I needed to find someone in whom I could confide to help me to understand *why* I should stay or to feel like I belonged. Although the school had arranged for a mentor to help me with the transition into the school, I needed someone to mentor me beyond academic and curricular needs. I needed someone who could listen to, and try to understand, my personal feelings. Fortunately there were three other people of color hired the same year I was hired. With a couple of these colleagues, I found brief chats expanding into conversations that filled my breaks. With my voice being shared on a personal level, I felt a little more complete—less different or out of place.

My most trusted confidante, chair of the modern and classical languages department, was appointed by the head of school as chair of the diversity committee during my second year at the school. Both he and the head of school must have believed in me, as they recommended that I be sent to the 1996 NAIS People of Color Conference in Baltimore to represent the school.

I'll never forget calling my mother on the phone. As I dialed her number and listened to the phone ring, I kept asking myself, Why would the school want to send me? I had very little experience teaching in an independent school; I didn't know what to expect; I didn't want to be seen as the poster child for diversity at the school; and I was being asked to go there alone. I remember asking my mother about the qualifications I had. "Well, remember, Honey," she said, "you have been a person of color for almost 37 years."

Yes, I still chuckle when I think of her calm yet reassuring response. I did have some experience in that aspect, and, as usual, I trusted my Mom and my intuition. And I went for it.

The annual conference now holds such significance in my personal and school life that I need to go every year. As a result of attending this gathering, I have found support. Those of us at the conferences develop many friendships, create networks of professionals, share common experiences, dialogue in an open and honest manner, educate the educated, and gain numerous opportunities for personal and academic growth. Since my introduction to the conference, I have helped to arrange the opening events at the People of Color Conference in St. Louis 1997, served on the student conference faculty in San Juan in 1998, and co-chaired the student conference in San Francisco in 1999, and I returned to work with the students as co-chair in Nashville in 2000.

Hard work and resolute courage have carried me through this 5-year transition from questioning and difficulty to having inclusive goals and clear vision. Hard work and resolute courage are gifts from the Great Spirit that I have grown to rely on and cherish. My school does have its problems, but the positives far outweigh the negatives. It is a wonderful community in which I have a meaningful place. Spiritually, I feel blessed to be working in a place where I do what I love and I love what I do. I trust and believe in my school, so much that I have allowed it to educate and nurture my own children. Ultimately, I am there because of the young people that benefit from its many educational and social opportunities. I remain the observer and listener, as I am trying to learn all I can from this opportunity. I look forward to the day when I can take what I have learned from this experience back home "to help my people."

Findings from a National Survey of Teachers of Color and from Analysis of the NAIS Database

Pearl Rock Kane and Alfonso J. Orsini

At best, independent schools have been only moderately successful at recruiting faculty of color.[1] *The NAIS Statistics*[2] report faculty of color as 8.4% of the independent school teaching force (among an undetermined sample of core member schools), up from 4% in 1987. While the percentage of teachers of color is slowly increasing, is this the best we can expect? As of July 2000, people of color constituted almost 29% of the total U.S. population, according to the U.S. Census Bureau.[3] In this section, we report the results of two surveys: (1) teachers of color in independent schools, and (2) teacher recruitment agencies. We surveyed both current teachers of color and recruitment organizations to try to determine which factors at independent schools most strongly attract or repel candidates of color. Given the disparity between the national population of color and the population of teachers of color at independent schools, this information could prove vital in understanding how to attract teachers of color to independent schools. Our aim is to determine which factors in the environment of independent schools and within schools themselves correlate most strongly with the presence of teachers of color. Later in the chapter, we also report demographic findings on NAIS schools in relation to teachers of color.

A NATIONAL SURVEY OF TEACHERS OF COLOR
IN INDEPENDENT SCHOOLS

The Sample

A total of 691 teachers responded to our survey.[4] Two-thirds of the respondents were female and one-third were male. Racially and ethnically, the background of respondents was African American (59%), Asian (17%), Hispanic (14%), biracial (7%), Middle Eastern (1%), and Native American (1%). The responses were close to the distribution of teachers of color in independent schools, according to 1997 NAIS statistics. Thirty percent were under 30 years of age, 27% were between 31 and 40, and 28% were over 40 years of age. Eighty-two percent of those responding worked in day schools, 4% in boarding schools, and 14% in schools that were a combination of day and boarding. Seventy-five percent of the schools were coeducational. Again, these values are close to national independent school norms.

Who Are the Teachers of Color Currently Working in NAIS Schools?

The self-reports of teachers of color working in independent schools define a profile of an independent school teacher of color as one who is likely to have grown up in a middle-class family, graduated from a private college or university with a GPA of 3.3, and incurred a debt of under $20,000. This profiled teacher is 20 times more likely to have attended an independent secondary school than the average person schooled in America.

Of nearly 500 respondents who discussed college finances, 38% reported family assistance, 32% reported scholarships, and only 29% relied on loans and other financial aid. If this survey is representative of teachers of color in NAIS schools today, over 60% represent themselves as middle class or higher.

It is hardly surprising that there was a statistically significant relationship between the level of debt and plans to leave teaching. As respondents' debt level increased, they were significantly ($\alpha = .001$) more likely to plan to leave teaching, citing their reasons as low salary and poor benefits.

How Did They Find Their Jobs?

Fifty-two percent of the respondents indicated that previous interaction with the school led them to their first teaching position. Newspaper job advertisements (15%), teacher placement agencies (10%), college placement offices (8%), faculty of color organizations (7%), and job fairs (6%) also figured into finding the first independent school teaching job. The academic level of students (47%) and the absence of requirements for teacher certification (24%) were cited most frequently as incentives to working in an independent school. The location of the school (33%), having a personal link to the school (25%), the feeling of support from the head of school (24%), the school's commitment to diversity (21%), and the receptivity of teachers at the school (20%) were the attractions to the current school of employment.

Are Teachers of Color Likely to Stay?

Most respondents (65%) were employed at their current school for 5 years or less, although 52% of respondents had more than 6 years of teaching experience. The overwhelming majority (86%) of teachers plan to stay in teaching, but not necessarily at the school of current employment. The reasons given for considering leaving the school were related to issues of diversity—wanting to work in a school with more teachers and students of color (20%) and a feeling of isolation (9%)—but job advancement (19%) and the desire for a more supportive administration (8%), which may or may not be related to being a person of color, also figured into reasons for considering changing schools. For the small percentage of teachers planning to leave teaching altogether (5%), low salary and the desire for advancement were cited most frequently.

One of the findings that proved to be statistically significant ($\alpha = .001$) is the relationship between intention to leave the current school for another independent school and the school's collaboration with public schools. Respondents working in independent schools that collaborated with public schools were less likely to consider leaving their school.

Demands Placed on Teachers of Color

When respondents were asked, "As a person of color, do you feel you have more demands placed on you than other teachers?" fully 59% said "yes" and 5% said "sometimes." The greatest burdens placed on teachers of color responding to the survey involve the expectation of supporting all students and parents of color (26%), the pressure to be "perfect" to negate stereotypes (22%), being expected to be the spokesperson/expert for one's race (20%), and coordinating diversity work, including educating the community about diversity (18%).

Both my parents were public school teachers who believed in the value and importance of good public schools, but they understood and supported my decision to teach at Penn Charter School, an independent school in Philadelphia. Teaching there allowed me to provide the best education available for my own children. I also knew that many independent schools are full of students poised to become tomorrow's leaders. As a person of color teaching at Penn Charter School I would be in a position to contribute to students' moral development and their sense of social justice. I wanted that opportunity.

I grew up in the small midwestern town of Davenport, Iowa. In those days Davenport had a predominantly German Jewish population. My father was the first African American teacher in Davenport's history. He knew what it was like to be placed under a magnifying glass of "standards" and to be watched closely in order to be judged "fit" for the job. He worked hard and earned trust and respect from the principal and, in fact, from the entire educational community. At the time of his death, he was honored by having the high school football stadium named after him.

From the time I was a very young child, my father always told me that I had to be better than my White colleagues and he was willing to do just about anything to help me be better. He was living proof of where such commitment could lead. He was my role model. In my first year of teaching at Penn Charter, I took my father's advice to heart, believing that a priority was to establish my academic credibility. I read everything I could get my hands on. I observed the older, more seasoned veterans. I prepared meticulously each day and never went to class unprepared. New African American faculty, no matter how well educated, no matter how well prepared, are frequently subject to the unfair scrutiny of White parents who question their command of the subject matter and their ability to communicate it to students.

The bottom line for parents in their questioning is always getting into a "good" college. No parents ever openly challenged my command of the subject matter, but there were those who challenged the appropriateness of the material. One parent left a note on my desk saying that a particular unit was wonderful but more appropriate for a high school student than for a sixth grader. Six years later when her son graduated, that parent left me another note expressing her gratitude for all that I had helped her son to accomplish and for not compromising my standards for anyone. To this day, I continue to perfect my craft. I was and remain generally overprepared, doing much more than any daily lesson plan requires.

Cheryl Irving
William Penn Charter School, PA

Attracting and Retaining Teachers of Color

Respondents were asked, "What do independent schools need to do to recruit more teachers of color?" There were almost 700 responses, over half of which offered different approaches to recruiting. One respondent summed up the general sentiment by saying, "Recruit actively and creatively and don't just give lip service to recruiting." The suggestions included the more familiar forms of recruiting such as contacting colleges, particularly African American colleges and universities, targeting teachers of color through agencies, and attending job fairs. Others suggested using "nontraditional approaches": advertising in people of color publications, recruiting at "nonpremiere" colleges, recruiting through churches and community centers, recruiting alumni, creating a pool of substitutes of color, sending teachers of color to do the recruiting, and using networks of parents of color at the school.

Other respondents talked about the need for structural changes such as reflecting the goal of diversity in the mission statement, engaging board support, deciding why the school should become diverse, and having a plan—a vision for diversity.

When respondents were asked, "What do independent schools need to do to recruit more teachers of color?" there were 955 suggestions, with 73% focusing on demonstrating a commitment to diversity at the school. Specific suggestions included offering professional support and mentoring, having more administrators of color, giving teachers of color a more powerful voice, admitting more students of color, creating a critical mass of teachers of color, including multicultural events in the curriculum, and offering racial sensitivity workshops for the entire school community, including students, staff, faculty, administration, and trustees.

Among other suggestions offered for recruitment, the following figured most prominently: improving salary and benefits, providing professional development, defining job expectations, and providing an inviting atmosphere.

Our school has the veneer of being extremely friendly. Cheery "hellos" abound. People pass each other in the halls and exchange banal chit chat: "How was your weekend?" " Do you have a nice group of kids this year?" This makes for a pleasant working atmosphere, but after several lunches in the teachers' lounge, I quickly realized that most teachers and staff are good friends, not passing acquaintances. They get together after school and on weekends. Many take family trips together over the summer. Sometimes, sitting in the lounge they continued their closely knit conversations as if I wasn't there. Finally I stopped going to the teachers' lounge. I felt it's okay to be a part of the group as long as I stay on the periphery. Because I smile each day people say, "She is always so upbeat and friendly," and they don't know how lonely I feel. They don't know that the extra effort I've made to get to know the children I teach is exactly the same effort I wish someone would extend to me. Until that happens, I will continue to feel like I am on the outside, looking in. Maybe one day someone will ask me in to sit at the table.

Kay Garth-Lee
Polytechnic School, CA

Concerning Directors of Diversity

Not surprisingly, the mere presence of a director of diversity in a school was not significantly related (a =.8) to the number of teachers of color in a school. As indicated several times in our research, the commitment of the entire community, and especially the administration, is critical for the attraction of teachers of color. The structural response of creating a director of diversity position in the absence of cultural changes is unlikely to alter the picture of diversity within a school. A single, unsupported position may create only symbolic diversity. To achieve the goal of faculty diversity, change must be systemic.

Increasing Numbers of People of Color

In our studies, the number of students of color significantly predicted the number of teachers of color in the school ($a = .001$). Again, this is supported by data from other sources. Increased numbers of people of color in a community have a greater chance to impact the cultural understandings of that community.[5] While the initial steps toward diversity are never easy, the changes become self-sustaining. More students of color attract more teachers of color who in turn attract more students of color.

Paralleling the finding that collaboration with public schools makes teachers of color less likely to want to leave their present school, this same collaboration was found to significantly predict the total number of teachers of color employed ($a = .002$) and students of color enrolled ($a = .001$). Public school collaboration may signal a general openness to greater community involvement and appears not only to attract people of color to a school, but also to help retain them. Collaboration with public schools may alleviate some of the isolation about which independent school teachers of color complain. This isolation, or exclusivity in its negative sense, may exacerbate the problem of becoming a more diverse school.

A SURVEY OF RECRUITMENT AGENCIES AND ORGANIZATIONS

To enhance our knowledge of issues in the attraction and retention of teachers of color, we approached 20 recruitment agencies and organizations, of which 12 responded. While this number is small, each of the respondents had worked with hundreds of candidates of color, and so their responses were based on extensive experience. These respondents included major commercial agencies, small one-person operations, and collaboratives of schools. When we asked these recruiters, "In your experience, has a profile of the successful candidate of color for independent school teaching emerged?" five key characteristics recurred in their responses:

- college attended ("Ivy League," "Strong," "Known")—9
- attended an independent school—7
- not too ethnic—5
- fit in (not rock boat, not ruffle feathers)—5
- middle-class background—3

Recruiters expressed their frustration with what seems to them to be too rigid a profile, and when asked to give independent schools a grade (on a scale of 1 to 100) on their "willingness to hire teachers of color," assigned an average grade of 54. When asked whether they thought independent schools were fully utilizing the pool of candidates of color, 11 of 12 responded "no." When asked what percentage of qualified candidates they thought they were reaching, eight of the 12 respondents stated a percentage below 50%. Asked what they would do to recruit more teachers of color if they had more resources, seven of the 12 stated that they would do more on-campus recruiting at colleges, and three stated that they would advertise more extensively. When they were asked about what makes a school attractive or unattractive to a candidate of color, their most frequent responses were as follows:

- diversity of student body
- diversity of faculty
- atmosphere/environment of school
- school's commitment to diversity
- respect given to faculty (autonomy, voice)
- salary/benefits

A STUDY OF THE NAIS DATABASE

After hearing from NAIS teachers of color and the recruitment agencies and organizations, we realized that we should try to more carefully study the hypotheses that are so often advanced about why some schools are more successful in their attempts to recruit and retain diverse faculty. The annual NAIS statistics present important aggregate statistics and averages, but figures such as the 1997 NAIS statistic of 7% teachers of color, when the study was conducted, did not reveal much about individual schools and reasons some are more diverse than others. Thus, we decided to look more closely at the specific internal and demographic factors at NAIS schools that might be associated with greater faculty diversity.

Discounting schools in Hawaii, the U. S. Territories,[6] and the 80 schools that did not respond to the NAIS survey on diversity issues, we examined 865 mainland NAIS schools. We were surprised to find that among these schools, the median percentage of teachers of color proves to be 4.26. Thus, at the median school no more than one in 20 teachers on staff would be a person of color. More shockingly, we learned

- 233 schools (or 27%) had not one teacher of color on staff
- 44% had no more than one teacher of color on staff
- 47% had no African American teachers,
- 50% had no Hispanic/Latino teachers, and
- 65% had no Asian/Pacific Islander teachers

The above suggest that many NAIS students may never work with a teacher of color over the course of their precollege studies. On the other hand, of the many "other" school employees that NAIS students will come in contact with (the maintenance staff, secretaries, security, and dining room people designated as "other" by NAIS), approximately 20% will be people of color. Consider the conception of people of color that such an experience will shape in the minds of NAIS students. Now picture these same students at around 40 years old, at the height of their careers in the U.S. work force in 2025, when people of color are projected to constitute 38% of the U.S. population. This may explain why the study conducted by NAIS in 1991 found that 47% of parents with incomes over $100,000 who were polled said that they would not send their children to "private" schools because they wanted them to have a diverse, real-world experience.[7]

WHICH SCHOOLS ARE LIKELY TO BE MORE DIVERSE?

To study which factors at NAIS schools might be most closely associated with faculty diversity, we gathered data on several internal variables at schools, including endowment, tuition levels for first, sixth, and twelfth grades, starting and median salaries, school size, percentage of students of color, and percentage of financial aid devoted to students of color. Among these, the factors that showed the highest correlation with the percentage of teachers of color on staff were starting salary, median salary, percentage of financial aid to students of color, and percentage of students of color at the school.[8]

Both the Teacher of Color Survey and the Recruitment Agency/Organization Survey suggest that the school's commitment to diversity is a major factor in attracting candidates of color to an independent school, an assertion that seems to be confirmed by the high correlation of percentage of students of color and percentage of financial aid to students of color with percentage of faculty of color.

A STUDY OF DEMOGRAPHICS IN INDEPENDENT SCHOOL ENVIRONMENTS

To look at demographic variables in the areas around the schools, we used the Census Bureau data on zip codes.[9] With these data, we were able to determine all of the following for both the zip code and the 20-mile radius of each of the 865 NAIS schools:

- total population
- percentage of population who live in urban, farm, or rural/nonfarm areas

- race/ethnicity of population
- percentage people of color in the population
- median family income
- median house price

Among these features, the ones that were most strongly associated with percentage of teachers of color in the schools were total population, percentage of urban population, and percentage of people of color in the population.[10] Thus, it seems that, to some extent, a school's ability to diversify staff is associated with its location, a finding that is corroborated by the 33% of respondents to the Teacher of Color Survey who cited location as a major factor in why they chose to work at their current schools. In general, the more diverse schools are located in more urban, more diverse, and more densely populated areas. This conclusion is borne out also by common sense and experience, which tell us that it is a much more difficult odyssey for a person of color to venture into a remote, largely White, rural area where there is no guarantee of a community of color.

FEATURES AT SCHOOLS WITH HIGHER AND LOWER FACULTY DIVERSITY

We also gained insight into the factors most strongly associated with faculty diversity by comparing means of internal and demographic features at schools with different levels of faculty diversity. Although we looked at many different levels of diversity, it will suffice here to juxtapose the conditions at schools with less than the NAIS median of 4.26% teachers of color, schools with 12 to 19.99% teachers of color, and schools with more than 20% teachers of color. Table 3.1 graphically depicts the key differences between these higher and lower diversity schools.

Clearly, the 26 schools with greater than 20% teachers of color tend to be located in more urban, more densely populated, and more diverse areas, which would explain their higher median family income and house value, as well as the higher starting and median salaries. We should note, however, that in the higher cost of living areas, the slight increases in salaries may not represent much in actual dollars. The more telling features are clearly those within the schools. The more diverse schools, which tend to be smaller, seem to be devoting a much greater percentage of financial aid to students of color, even though they have much lower mean endowments. They are therefore attracting more students of color and perhaps, as indicated by our survey respondents, more teachers of color. They also proved to be attracting more paying students of color. Indeed, despite the significance of financial aid to students

Table 3.1. Means of Internal and External Variables at Schools with Various Levels of Faculty Diversity.

Variable	Less Than 4.26% Teachers of Color (n = 435)	Greater Than 12% Teachers of Color (n = 121)	Greater Than 20% Teachers of Color (n = 26)
Total Population (zip code radius)	20,566	31,329	32,954
Percent of People of Color in Population	13%	26%	32%
Percent of Urban Population	66%	92%	96%
Median Family Income	$51,374	$56,963	$57,550
Median House Price	$170,953	$274,506	$310,389
Number of Students	416	408	274
Number of Teachers	47	46	29
Percent of Financial Aid to Students of Color	27%	49%	52%
Percent of Students of Color	10.3%	21.3%	26.2%
Endowment	$13 million	$10.8 million	$2.5 million
Starting Salary	$20,762	$22,871	$23,596
Median Salary	$30,533	$35,225	$34,250

of color in trying to diversify faculties, we should remember that only around a third of students of color at NAIS schools receive aid.

IMPLICATIONS AND RECOMMENDATIONS FOR ACTION

The arguments for diversifying NAIS faculties are numerous and compelling. What, we ask, can our research offer to those many schools that have tried earnestly to diversify or to those that now want to begin diversifying their faculties?

First, it seems clear that a critical mass of students of color is key in attracting teachers of color. It is also evident that a greater commitment of financial aid may be the surest way to attract students of color.

Second, to build more diverse faculties, independent schools may need to stretch their conceptions of the ideal independent school teacher, especially of the ideal teacher of color, and recruit more broadly. If, as the recruiters suggest, independent school administrators have come to view the ideal teacher of color as a middle-class person who attended independent school and a private competitive college and who, thus, will not "rock the boat," then it is time for us to rethink the ideal.

Third, independent schools have to be aware of the inordinate demands, both implicit and explicit, that are being placed on teachers of color—demands that can make their work lives untenable at school.

Fourth, as far as recruitment practices are concerned, it has been established that candidates of color are influenced positively in their decisions to teach at a given school by the teachers that they meet. Also, we have learned through past studies[11] that among Columbia and Barnard students surveyed, students of color particularly said that they would be positively influenced by on-campus recruitment. Thus, as the survey suggested, independent schools need to do more campus recruiting themselves, especially by sending to college campuses current independent school teachers who can share their own positive experiences with prospective teachers. Furthermore, since over half of current teachers of color in independent schools found their jobs through some affiliation with the school, administrators need to make the most of networking to find new teachers of color. Consulting students and parents and current teachers of color when openings arise and making connections with churches, social service organizations, and nearby public schools, are suggested approaches.

Finally, while it may be true that independent schools in urban areas tend to have more diverse faculties, geography does not guarantee diversity. The true make or break issue of hiring teachers of color may be the human factor. Independent school leaders may need to re-evaluate the climate and atmosphere of their schools. Is the school truly a welcoming place where diversity is tangibly honored? The human connection that is offered or not offered when a new person enters the school may be the single most critical element in efforts to recruit teachers of color. Will a candidate entering the school be greeted with warmth and acceptance and interest, or with a posture of exalted scrutiny? If the latter, then even a school in the heart of New York or Los Angeles may have trouble diversifying. If the former is the case, and if a school connects significantly with the outside larger community and with people of color, then faculty diversity may be an attainable ideal after all.

Struggles and Rewards

Reveta Bowers
The Center for Early Education, CA

Have you ever walked into a room and immediately felt out of place? Did you have on the wrong attire? Had you come dressed casual for an event everyone else knew was business attire? Those were the feelings I expected to experience moving from an inner-city public school to an independent school for the first time in 1972. I was at the time a young Black woman, on my way to embracing an African American identity before eventually joining others under the umbrella of "People of Color."

I came to teaching as a profession reluctantly in the first place. I was following in the firmly established footprints of a grandmother, mother, and two aunts who had been and were teachers in public schools. Although hesitant at first to believe that I had found "my calling," I discovered in that first inner-city classroom a real joy in working with the kids. What I found joyless and burdensome was the system. That lack of affinity for crowded classes, deficient physical plants, stressed faculty and staff, and uninspired materials led me to follow the advice of an administrator in the system and interview at the independent school her daughter attended.

That is how in August 1972, I scheduled an interview with the director of a small West Los Angeles private school. That interview, and the subsequent offer of a job team-teaching in a kindergarten class, led to what has become a 30-year adventure, for I am still in that school today.

What was it like to go teach at a largely White, upper- and upper-middle-class private school in 1972? How hard was it to be the first Black teacher? There were two people who were largely responsible for my successful transition. One was the woman who hired me and quickly became a trusted mentor, teacher, and advisor. She had come to the school the year before me to found the elementary division of what had been established in 1939 as a well-regarded nursery school and later an accredited teacher training college. She was articulate and persuasive about all of the reasons I should consider moving to this newly started elementary division.

My team-teaching partner was the other person who so aided me in effecting my entry into the world of private schools. Our backgrounds could not have been more different. While I had just left an inner-city public school system, this was to be her first teaching position after leaving the convent! Both of us, misfits in the beginning, quickly united in our desire to be a fully functioning, successful team in this new place. To this day, I attribute a great deal of my success as a person of color in an independent school to the philosophy of team-teaching embraced by the school and to my pairing with that first teacher.

For those children and the children who would follow them, I was the first and perhaps only Black teacher they would experience in their early education. Having been educated in public schools, except for university, I was unused to the level of participation, interest, involvement, and, at times, interference of parents.

I found myself working, as I had in school, to prove all over again that I was well educated, articulate, and skilled enough to meet their expectations. I once again remembered what my mother had always told me as I entered a new class in school or competed for something as the first or one of very few minorities in school. "You have to be better than the others," she would say. "You have to try harder, work faster, and exceed people's expectations!"

As a minority, there are never times that you can afford to forget your difference unless you're surrounded by family. Over time, others may be able to see you for who you are rather than as a member of a minority group, but that journey from awareness to tolerance to hoped for acceptance sometimes can be a long and frustrating one. But if there is one thing I have learned in my 30-year stint as an independent school teacher and school head, it is that it must be two-way. If I want others to be aware of me, I must be aware of who they are. If I want tolerance, I must be tolerant myself, and if I want acceptance, I must be accepting.

Throughout my career, I and many others have battled being stereotyped and perpetuating stereotypes. I have worked toward being accepted not as a member of an ethnic group, but as an individual.

The most intriguing and, at times, the most challenging part of my job has been helping young children to see the world unfettered by biases, prejudices, or opinions of others. Children are never "color blind," as many would choose to believe. One of the first things we teach them to do as toddlers is to discriminate. We teach them the difference between big and little, hot and cold, hard and soft, black and white. It is the adults who shade those concepts with meaning. The intent of the young child in most situations is to simply seek answers. With children, it is easy to trust in their innocence and the simplicity they require when they question: "Why is your hair different?" "Why are you that color?" In my first year teaching at my school, one of my favorite students extended an invitation to dinner at his home. This endearing 5-year-old proudly issued the invitation and promptly assured me I would love the meal. Beaming, he said, "We're going to have ribs and watermelon!"

Will you encounter prejudice and people who will never accept you in an independent school? Probably. But for those who do not, there are many more who will value your professionalism, your personal integrity, and what you give their children and families. Each new child, parent, colleague, and person in the school community represents an opportunity to whom you can tell your story and, in turn, to hear theirs. For every parent in a parent–teacher conference who resented a young, inexperienced, Black woman delivering unwelcome news about his or her child, there were numerous others who were grateful for the observations and counsel of a teacher they had come to believe was skilled and cared deeply about her students. For every person I heartily disliked, I have loved so many others.

In 30 years, I have been privileged to work with and for really wonderful people. The increasingly diverse families, faculty, staff, and boards in my school have worked with me to sustain a school community in which all kinds of people can be valued and nurtured. My responsibility toward that diversity, particularly as a person of color, is to model inclusion, tolerance for views that differ from my own, and acceptance. I am obligated to mentor and encourage new teachers and administrators, as I was mentored and encouraged early in my career. Our schools must be places where every teacher is welcomed for the qualities and qualifications that potentially will make him or her a valued and respected faculty member. Each stereotype that we dispel about a person of color, a religion, a sexual orientation, or a socioeconomic status, eases the transition and makes diversity an achievable, not just laudable, goal.

If you're reading this book, you're probably also a member of or interested in being a part of an independent school community. If you're also a person of color, as I am, do not expect that membership to be without discomfort. You will never forget or lose your feeling of being different. The learning curve is often steep and prone to emotional volatility. But what you potentially represent is the opportunity to teach life lessons that are enduring and important. Mary Pipher in her wonderful book, *The Shelter of Each Other*, talks about the necessity for people to have and experience "meaningful work" in their lives. My career in an independent school has been some of the most positive, meaningful work in my life. My wish for you is that it can be in yours as well.

Excess Baggage

Alexis Wright
Rye Country Day School, NY

As I slowly navigated my rusting 12-year-old car into the exclusive independent prep school's parking lot, I discovered that I was surrounded by a sea of
expensive foreign vehicles, each one looking newer, sleeker, and shinier than
the next. I parked and slowly got out of my car, making sure that my door
would not even come close to touching the side of the Mercedes to the left
of me. It was at that distinct point, despite excitement that had been brew-
ing in me, that I considered turning around and not appearing for my 8 a.m.
interview. Based solely on that view of the parking lot, I knew for sure that I
would be uncomfortable working in such an overwhelmingly affluent environment. And to me, affluent meant that there would be a lot of rich, snobby
White people around; I was sure that people of color were not driving those
cars and dropping their kids off, unless they were the chauffeurs. I paused,
but based on phone conversations, this school really wanted to interview me
and I felt I had much to offer, so I continued on. Lots of thoughts ran through
my mind as I walked through the parking lot and toward the main building
on that cold, snowy February morning: my academic achievements in college
and graduate school, my experience with children and coaching sports, and
what I would say to the head of school to really impress him. With my confidence brimming, I felt for sure that I would be able to win a job at this school,
even if it meant battling these initial feelings of being out of place. How long
would those feelings last? No more than a few days, I was sure.

Suddenly, those thoughts were brought to a dead stop by what I can still
vividly remember 6 years later as one of the most surreal and disturbing sights
I have ever seen. Not only were the expensive cars parked in the parking lot,
but they also were lined up in front of the entrance to the main building. Each
parent behind the wheel of those cars was taking turns dropping off a child
for school. The children seemed to joyfully tumble out of the cars, happy to
be at school and happy to start the day. But it was not that sight that shocked
me the most.

It was witnessing an African American male who was opening the car
doors in the procession and letting forth with what seemed to me to be the
deepest, most booming "Good morning!" I had ever heard, to each and every

71

child. The parents looked as if they were pleased to see him, but, more important, looked as if they were pleased to have someone open their car doors for them. The children greeted the African American doorman and ran into the school. It seemed to be an arrangement that worked, and judging by the huge smile on the doorman's face, it was an arrangement that was fine with him. To me, however, it seemed like I had been transported back in time. To me, the scene looked like something out of a minstrel show. To me, I saw a jolly Black man who was happy being a doorman to privilege. I saw a servant who was opening car doors and welcoming these White kids into school, a school where I was to spend the morning selling myself in hopes of getting a job offer.

Most of my schooling had been in public schools, and so my assumptions of life at an independent school came largely from stereotypes I had developed from reading stories and watching movies. Spoiled rich White kids in crisp blue blazers and pleated skirts would go to class in ivy covered buildings, thus being prepared for their admission to highly selective colleges and a guaranteed place of prominence in society. This stereotype also included visions of these kids playing sports foreign to me, like field hockey and lacrosse on huge expanses of grass during the afternoons. And in my mind, while the teachers in the classroom might be White men in tweed coats and bow ties, the staff that would facilitate this privileged lifestyle by serving food, cleaning hallways, and opening car doors, would be people of color. Without stepping foot into the school and only observing the environment from the outside, I felt all of these stereotypes were about to be proven correct, and here was a Black man affirming my suspicions. And thus, here was my introduction to searching for a job in the independent school world.

As I went through the interview process that day, I still could not get rid of the sight of that Black man opening car doors and greeting the White students. That image hung over me all day, making it difficult to concentrate on the interview with the school's faculty. It made me bitter and angry; in my mind the racist administration of the school clearly saw that Black people did not belong in the classroom and that they were only fit for opening doors and serving as the welcoming committee. Perhaps later in the day this man would be lucky enough to mop some hallways as well. As an African American male myself, I wondered exactly what my responsibilities might entail at the school should I be offered a job. I certainly did not see any other people of color in the school as I made the interview rounds that day, and I saw very few students of color as well. Clearly, this was an environment that did not value people of color, and I knew immediately that I would never consider an offer of any kind for employment from this school.

Reflecting on that experience a few years later, my anger has long abated, and I now realize that the thoughts I had formulated that day were based on quick observations and an even quicker mental calculus, both heavily fueled by pre-existing stereotypes about independent schools and, on a larger level, about American society. Growing up as an African American male in America, one is bombarded with various images related to race and class; all of those experiences served to color and influence my perception of the events on that day. A few weeks after this incident I was hired by another independent school and found myself coaching a baseball game against the school where I had gone for that initial interview. It was there that I discovered that the man who was opening car doors and greeting students was not forced into what I had deemed to be a subservient role by the "racist" administration at the school. In fact, this person happened to be a physical education teacher, and according to job descriptions at some suburban independent schools (including the one where I currently work), it is the physical education teachers who open car doors for students and greet them upon their arrival at school. Because of my background and frame of reference, however, it is not hard for me to imagine that the assumptions I made back then would be similar to ones that other people of color might make if they approached that independent school on that cold February day.

It is always difficult to speak for others, but if I extrapolate from my experience, it would seem that the outward appearances of a school matter tremendously and can act as a hindrance to recruiting candidates of color to teach. The instant I saw the man opening the car doors, I knew I would never work in that school. By the time I realized what his role really was, it was too late, and presumably one school that had showed some interest in further diversifying its faculty had missed an opportunity. Administrators need to be sensitive to outward appearances and the way actions by their staff may be perceived, just as candidates of color need to realize that there may be more than meets the eye. I was guilty of making a knee-jerk reaction, but this particular school was also guilty of not realizing how outsiders might interpret the use of its staff.

For me, teaching in a predominantly White independent school has meant constantly challenging people's perceptions and battling assumptions, both my own and those of others around me. There are events that happen almost every day, which I may perceive one way, and another person will interpret in a different manner. This happens all the time, but when the perceptions and assumptions deal with race, the significance and ramifications can be much more severe and disturbing. For example, if I am complimented for being articulate one more time, I may jump out of a window! To me and to many of my friends of color, being called articulate is code for, "I was expecting you to speak using double negatives and slang, like you just walked in from the street." The assumption is that proper English is not expected, but why should it not be? An assumed innocent compliment from a White person has now turned into an insult, which the teacher probably was not aiming to deliver. I've had teachers ask me to speak to and mentor students of color who are in academic or social trouble, with the underlying assumption being that because the student and I might have the same skin color, then surely I can make a connection that others have not been able to make. Never mind that the student may have a totally different background from mine, or may be in a different division of the school, or that I have a full schedule and my own advisees to worry about. Our race might be the only common denominator, but it is assumed that all problems will be solved.

The biggest problem I have had to forge my way through has been battling the assumptions of some coworkers that I am favored by the school's administration and get whatever I ask for, from support for professional development opportunities to promotions. The mental strains of dealing with these assumptions and uncertainties on a daily basis have taken their toll. Hearing comments made to my face and behind my back has been damaging, and at times has made me evaluate my commitment to my school and to independent school teaching. The comments have even made me question my own success: Is it due to my efforts or am I just a token being promoted as the school's commitment to diversity? As a result, I have had to develop coping mechanisms and cultivate my own support system, something I believe most White faculty do not need to do. If White faculty do need such a support system, chances are they may not have to look any further than others in their own school for it. When there are so few people of color in an independent school, support systems are hard to develop within the boundaries of that environment.

Based on my experiences, it is my assumption that many independent schools do not consider that teachers of color will need additional support once they have been hired and placed in the classroom. As independent schools try to diversify their faculty and student bodies, the solution is not as easy as simply placing teachers and students in the school so that they may be referred to as shining examples of diversity. As minority students adjust to schools with cultures and traditions that may be vastly different from what they have grown up with, some independent schools are acting to meet their needs in several ways. Peer support groups, clubs, and counselors try and help these students adjust to their new environment and new school culture. In contrast, what are the existing structures that are available to help minority teachers cope as they adjust to their new surroundings? I do not know of any schools that have such programs in place.

In lieu of any such program at my school, throughout the past few years I have reached out to other teachers of color at surrounding schools in order to establish my own personal network. This action was a direct result of my not having anyone in the school environment whom I felt truly comfortable talking with about various incidents that had happened. For example, as a new teacher, I had no idea what the faculty response would be if I applied for a grant to go to the National Association of Independent Schools' People of Color Conference (POC). I had no one I felt comfortable talking with about this, so I opted for the easy solution, which was not to go. I attended the conference the next year, however, and the reactions from some fellow faculty members ranged from legitimate queries about what the conference was about, to a White teacher wondering whether White people were allowed to attend, to ignorant remarks about why there even would need to be a gathering of people of color in the first place. I went to the following year's conference as well, and this time another teacher of color from my school joined me. Of course, the response from other faculty was that we were leaving for a vacation, and that the conference really could not serve any important purpose. What a demoralizing feeling it was to be diminished by fellow faculty for going to an academic conference. Would other faculty have been subjected to the same disdain and questioning about their opportunities to attend a conference? I do not think so.

When my colleague and I returned from the POC Conference, one of the first things we did was share our experiences with the faculty. We talked honestly about the pressures of being a person of color in an independent school, both as a student and teacher. We talked about how being the "only one" is an isolating experience. Some of the teachers had realized that having only one student of color in a classroom might occasionally be awkward for the student, but they never realized that a faculty member might experience the same thing. I talked about how some of the same assumptions that are made about students of color had been levied at me by some of the faculty. For example, I was called "White" because of the way I dressed and the music I listened to when I was a student in middle school. I never imagined that 14 years later as a teacher in an independent school, I would hear the same comments directed at me by another teacher, but indeed I did. How does one cope with that type of comment? When our presentation was over, the response was overwhelming in terms of the accolades and apologies that we both received. While talking to people afterward, I realized that nobody had shared with them some of the pressures that students and faculty of color face in an independent school environment. Nobody had ever explained the benefits of having faculty of color in a school, or what it was like to attend a school function and realize that the only person of color there is you, except for the waiters. Nobody had told them what that feels like, what the embarrassment and frustration from thoughtless comments feel like.

I share this story to emphasize that it is not enough to hire faculty of color and expect all of them to thrive in the independent school world without providing any type of support. At the very least, administrators should present information about the People of Color Conference to new teachers of color and guarantee assistance if the faculty member chooses to attend. Actively mentoring teachers of color throughout the year also might help cultivate longer relationships between teachers and their schools. Having open dialogues and honestly warning faculty of color about possible incidents that might occur are also good ideas. My experience was such that I did not have a mentoring relationship at my school, but I was able to forge relationships with White faculty members who were sensitive to some of the issues that people of color face in a predominantly White and affluent independent school. I also was able to take advantage of previous existing relationships with faculty of color at other schools for advice and, most important, for venting my anger. I found people to confide in, and I found White allies at my school who understood discussions of race. Yet again, I wonder if these are steps that White people ever have to take. The conclusion is that it is important to recognize that those options are not always available to everyone, and if administrators at schools expect to hire and retain faculty of color, it is to their advantage to make sure that resources are available for supporting and nurturing faculty of color. It is also critical to help educate the rest of the school community on issues of diversity, and this is where the role of a diversity coordinator can become important. A diversity coordinator who can have frank discussions with all faculty and students and monitor curriculum to make sure that it is inclusive and reflects the larger society we are a part of is invaluable. There will always be issues surrounding diversity, race, and class that come up, but having a point person devoted to addressing those issues within a school, for both faculty and students of color, can only be an asset as schools present themselves as inclusive and diverse environments to students, parents, and faculty. As a person of color in an independent school, the "excess baggage" that I have been forced to consistently carry around has taken its toll, but it also has inspired me to keep working to dispel myths and ignorant thoughts, and to realize why people of color are needed in independent schools. In an environment where the only people of color that students may see are the ones working as nannies, cafeteria workers, or custodians, teachers of color are professional role models for all students. Just as students of color should have an equal opportunity to turn to people who they feel can understand their situation in a predominantly White environment, it is as important to have a faculty that reflects our increasingly multicultural society. That is what I keep reminding myself when faced with assumptions, either those made by others or my own.

Best Practices: An Analysis of Teacher Diversity in Eleven New York City Independent Schools

*Kate Knopp, John Baldwin, John Barrengos,
Dennis Bisgaard, Marc Bogursky, Sidney Bridges,
Kathleen Brigham, Virginia Carnes, Tom Doar,
Kecia Hayes, Tracy Knox, Jerry Loewen, Gary Niels,
Kolia O'Connor, Cathleen Randall, and Jan Scott*

OBJECTIVES OF THE STUDY

To explore what independent schools have learned from their efforts to re-cruit and retain faculty of color, we designed a study of 11 New York City independent schools, aiming to incorporate a variety of perspectives. By ex-amining the results of interviews with heads of school, directors of diversity (or persons responsible for diversity or hiring faculty where diversity direc-tors were not designated positions in the school), and teachers of color, the study sought to gain a clear sense of "best practices."

We use the term "faculty of color" to mean any non-White member of the faculty. The definition does not imply that all faculty of color have similar experiences or professional needs. While this definition may risk polarizing perceptions of racial issues as only White and Black, our purpose was to col-lect the lessons learned from these schools' efforts to recruit and retain non-White faculty.

STRUCTURE OF THE STUDY

The 11 schools that were invited to participate all agreed to be a part of the study. They were selected to represent a variety of approaches to diversity, so that we might examine a wide perspective on recruiting and retaining faculty of color.

Contacts within each school were asked to set up interviews with four appropriate people, including the head of school, two teachers of color, and a person with a specific responsibility for diversity. (This study uses the term "director of diversity" for this category of respondents.) Our aim was to interview the person who works most directly with issues of diversity at the school. Titles ranged from director of institutional diversity to multicultural coordinator to head of mentoring program. If no such position existed, we sought out a dean of faculty or similar position who had influence in the hiring process. The study did not specify age or experience criteria. As a result, we interviewed teachers with a wide range of personal and professional experiences.

INTERVIEW PROTOCOLS

A team of 15 graduate student researchers designed three separate protocols to distill the lessons learned about hiring and retaining faculty of color from the three perspectives of the head, the director of diversity, and the teachers of color at the school. All of the student interviewers had previous teaching experience in independent schools. Considerable time was spent developing pivotal questions about school culture, hiring practices, and professional development for teachers of color.

THE INTERVIEWS

Four interview teams, composed of three graduate students each, conducted a full set of interviews at two different schools, and one team conducted interviews at three schools. A total of 43 interviews[1] were conducted over the 11 schools. Whenever possible, all interviews were conducted in person and on the same day, on the school's campus. Once four interviews at each school were completed, the team met to compare perceptions and collaborate on a report addressing the following points:

- the school's demographics, including type of school, number of teachers of color, staff of color, and location

- the school's commitment to recruiting and retaining teachers of color
- evidence of the commitment
- differences in perception among the people interviewed
- actual efforts to recruit and retain teachers of color
- successes and struggles
- what the team learned from doing this case study.

Case studies of each school provided the background for analyzing the interview data.

ANALYSIS OF THE DATA

The three sets of data were analyzed across three dimensions. The first two dimensions, *recruiting* and *retaining*, focused on what is currently happening in the schools and what techniques are most successful in recruiting and retaining teachers of color. The third dimension, *prospects and issues*, focused on what the three groups thought was needed to improve efforts to hire and retain faculty of color.

Questions from each of the three protocols were sorted as they pertained to each of the three dimensions. For example, two questions from the heads of school protocol specifically addressed issues of retention. Those two questions were then compared across the 11 interviews. Likewise, two questions from the directors of diversity protocol and two from the teachers of color protocol addressed retention issues. These, too, were compared across the interviews.

RECRUITING TEACHERS OF COLOR

Heads of School

Some schools have developed policies about hiring faculty of color. Does your school have such a policy? What is it? How did it originate? Is it effective?

Six of the 11 schools operate with some type of policy pertaining to the hiring of faculty of color. Four of the six generally adhere to a policy that there must be a person of color considered as a finalist for every opening the schools seek to fill. Only one of those four, however, considers that to be a formal policy clearly stated, written, and followed. Variations on the policy occur at two other schools. A fifth school has an informal policy stating that there must be at least one person of color in the applicant pool (not a finalist) for any job opening. If there are no applicants of color, the person in charge of hiring must explain why he or she could not recruit any applicants of color. At the time of the interview, the final school was in the process of developing a policy with input from its director of diversity, the board, parents, students, and teachers.

Four of the schools have no policy specific to hiring faculty of color. Two of those spoke of the need to standardize their hiring practices for *all* hiring, and one of those described a detailed protocol developed by the school with the help of a consultant: An administrative and staff team develop a list of qualities, characteristics, and skills needed for the job they are seeking to fill. If it is important to that initial team that the candidate be a person of color, this would become an item on the list. The head of school reserves the power to rank the items on the list. In the end, each list contains the criteria against which all candidates are measured. The last school with no formal policy spoke vaguely of its "efforts" and pointed to recent successes in hiring "young teachers from superior academic institutions."

It may be significant that only two of the 11 schools mentioned efforts to recruit and reach out to potential candidates of color in creative ways. Those schools spoke of targeting candidates of color with ads in newspapers with predominantly Black or Latino readerships. Only one school mentioned an initiative encouraging alumni/ae of color to return to the school to teach.

Directors of Diversity

Does the school actively recruit teachers of color? How does it do that? What else have you learned about hiring and holding on to teachers of color at this school?

Six of the 11 schools confidently answered "yes" when asked if they actively recruit teachers of color. All six cited the annual Diversity Resource Collaborative Teachers of Color Job Fair in New York City as evidence of their efforts.

Four directors of diversity responded cautiously and with obvious difficulty. One seemed resigned: "I don't know. There is a broad suggestion that we have a finalist of color but no one does much about it." Another said, "Recruit actively? Well, we go to the fair, but I don't think they've hired anyone from there, yet." Said a third, "Well, our school doesn't really want the kind of diversity you might find in candidates at the job fair. They'd rather recruit straight from Ivy League colleges." The general sentiment was that the schools talked a lot about hiring faculty of color, but that most schools were neither sufficiently aggressive nor strategic in their efforts to find candidates of color.

Teachers of Color

How did you come to this institution? A recruitment agency? Through other institutions? Why did you choose this school and it, you? Is the school committed to actively recruiting teachers of color?

The 21 responses to the first question conveyed how varied people's paths into the world of independent education could be. The breakdown was as follows: 2 responded with the help of an alumni/ae; 3 used the *New York Times*; 4 through professional contacts; 3 aided by friends or family; 3 utilized a recruiting agency; and 6 were beneficiaries of special recruitment. (In this case, special recruiting refers to job fairs for people of color, teacher of color recruitment agencies, or outside funding for an intern who found a full-time position.) Many of the schools' formal efforts to attract teachers of color were particularly successful with young teachers seeking initial employment. Experienced teachers seemed to find independent schools either through their own or their neighbors' children, or through professional contacts at conferences or in graduate school courses. A lower school principal convinced one woman (now a 17-year veteran of independent schools) to join the faculty by talking with her as she dropped her daughter off for school each morning. Another teacher had worked in the public school system and was befriended by a Teachers College classmate who invited her to visit an independent school. This teacher mentioned that the possibility of tuition remission for her son was an appealing offer to join independent education.

When teachers were asked if their schools actively recruited teachers of color, responses varied. Fifteen of the 21 responses fell somewhere between a definite "yes" and "no." The numbers were as follows: 5 responded "yes"; 9 declared, "The school says they are"; 6 stated they were "not sure"; and 1 stated "no." This confusion is a powerful statement, but the nature of the responses seemed to illuminate the complexities of the hiring processes.

Many teachers acknowledged that the schools seem to be trying, but admitted that efforts were sporadic and unsuccessful. For example, one teacher said, "I believe the school is looking to increase its faculty of color; however, it seems to happen randomly. Why, for example, isn't the director of diversity in charge of a strategic plan for hiring?" Another teacher offered, "The whole effort is unfocused; then when it fails, they say, 'You see, we tried, but the candidates are just not out there.'"

Several teachers looked to their heads of school and department chairs for their personal and professional commitment. The gatekeepers of the institution must believe that hiring faculty of color is a priority. "The head understands the issues and many of the staff are aware, so I am hopeful," offers one young teacher. "Department chairs have considerable voice, and so it's up to them," says another.

The bulk of the responses to, "Is the school committed to actively recruiting teachers of color?" addressed the issue of how to measure the commitment. The teachers seemed not to trust the words of school administrators who talked about a commitment to hire teachers of color.

- "I don't know. There are not many [teachers of color]. They do talk a lot about it, though."
- "They say they are, but little is being done."
- "They keep saying it. But I don't see proof."
- "Interested in . . . or committed? I'm not sure?"
- "Half-and-half. . . . Some people are committed. Some are afraid."

DISCUSSION OF DATA ON RECRUITING TEACHERS OF COLOR

There is little clarity around schools' policies for hiring faculty of color, and there exist very different perceptions about schools' efforts. Heads of schools say they are making efforts and some progress. Directors of diversity and teachers of color feel the efforts are, at best, unfocused and lacking in specific strategies. None of the groups seemed to know what the school's goals were relative to hiring teachers of color or how they ought to proceed.

Without exception (and often more forcefully), teachers of color had much more to say about schools' efforts to hire faculty of color than did heads. Teachers of color talked with great passion and at great length about how schools were shaping or not shaping their efforts.

While this is a small sample, it seems that most candidates find their way into independent schools through personal contacts and personal encounters with teachers from the school. Teachers committed to independent education who attend conferences and workshops, and are enrolled graduate courses, can increase the pool of candidates of color.

"Hiring is an art," said one head of school, "and is linked to retention issues." The people who work with new faculty ought to have significant influence in the hiring process, so that they feel in some way responsible for bringing candidates on board. That responsibility will become support on a daily basis. Schools need to examine and be reflective about their hiring procedure so that they might know how to better attract and hire faculty of color. The results of the interviews appear to underline the fact that present efforts to recruit faculty of color are made haphazardly, despite the rhetoric of commitment from the heads.

RETAINING TEACHERS OF COLOR

Heads of School

What kinds of orientation and ongoing support does your school provide for teachers new to your school? What kinds of professional support are specific to the needs of faculty of color?

Three of the 11 schools hold special orientations for teachers new to their institutions. Two other schools make a point of sending young teachers to the New York State Association of Independent Schools (NYSAIS) New Teachers Institute before they begin their first year in the classroom.

While all 11 school heads mentioned some type of mentoring system, only two schools either paid the mentor teachers for their work with younger teachers or provided "release time" for them to do the work. Two other schools had established mentor programs as part of their in-house professional development work, but considered them to be part of the daily work of teaching and offered no additional compensation. One mentorship program includes weekly seminars and guest speakers to support teacher training, but that program happens only in the lower school. Mentors regularly meet by themselves in one program, while first-year teachers do the same; the purpose is to keep both parties accountable to the process. Two heads mentioned the need for mentoring to be coupled with classroom visits and with some sort of teacher evaluation. In both cases, the relationship between mentoring and evaluation was not clearly delineated.

Ongoing discussion groups by grade-level teams of teachers or by departments seemed to be the second most frequently cited evidence of professional support. Nine of the 11 heads of school spoke about such meetings and discussion groups.

When asked about the specific needs of teachers of color, heads made several interesting observations in two general categories. Five suggested that since the needs of teachers of color are not uniform, the school could not address them as a group. The other six respondents addressed the question by stating that "retention issues are fundamentally linked to development of *people,* period." If people feel listened to and supported, personally and professionally, they will choose to stay at a school. One head spoke of the importance of "all staff to find colleagues they can trust," and suggested that "support lies largely in school culture." Another head thought first of the director of diversity as a key resource for teachers of color. "We have a multicultural coordinator, but we are more focused on new teachers in general so it's not necessary to do anything separate."

Two heads spoke persuasively of the need for teachers of color to have support systems outside the school and encouraged teachers of color to build personal and professional networks. Both listed numerous New York area resources: Interschool multicultural meetings, Seeking Educational Equity and Diversity (SEED) meetings, Diversity Resource Collaborative, and the NAIS People of Color Conference.

Directors of Diversity

What kinds of orientation does your school have for teachers who are new to your school? What kinds of professional support are specific to the needs of faculty of color? What else have you learned about hiring and holding onto teachers of color at this school?

The responses from directors of diversity closely paralleled those given by heads of school. Differences of opinion arose about the quality of the orientation programs. Nine of the 11 discussed the mentorship meetings and orientations as being "informal" or "not formal"; several talked about the tendency for "buddy systems" to "fizzle" by the middle of winter.

When asked which kinds of support have been most useful to teachers of color, seven described forums to discuss issues of diversity at the school. Several made a point of using daily issues of the school to engage the deeper issues of school culture. All emphasized the need for every person to feel that he or she has someone with whom to talk. The nature of the forums varied among schools and ranged in title: Diversity Committee, Respect Committee, Faculty Support Committee, the Valuing Differences Committee, and Diversity Dialogue. Some forums were multiracial, while others were designed expressly for teachers of color.

Five of the 11 directors of diversity noted the importance of contact networks outside the school. They mentioned the same networks noted by the heads and underscored the importance of encouraging faculty to take professional development time for themselves. Encouragement included providing substitutes for teachers of color while they engaged in professional development. This meant establishing an institutional priority for the professional development of teachers of color.

One director of diversity made a powerful point with regard to professional development for teachers of color. "When I came here 7 years ago, I took advantage of all the professional networks and opportunities. I chose to be involved in issues of diversity. I went to every gathering and conference I could. Two years ago I gave it up—the school never gave me a cent to do it and never encouraged me to make the effort to go. It feeds me, yes, but I already spend most of my time on school issues." While outside support seems important, it often is added on top of an already long list of activities and responsibilities.

Teachers of Color

In what ways have you been supported in your work at the school? Do you see a future for yourself at this school? Why or why not?

Fourteen of 21 teachers responding cited attending conferences and workshops and being given financial support for graduate study as the most accessible form of support. A school's willingness to send teachers to conferences or to pay for graduate courses is clearly understood and appreciated by teachers of color. It is not clear, however, whether these teachers felt most supported by conference experiences or whether they were choosing to define institutional "support" in an easily measured way.

Ten teachers mentioned that the mentoring program, including class visitations, was helpful, but they were more enthusiastic about support from colleagues and from the entire community. One teacher offered: "I've been supported in so many ways. I'm in continuous dialogue with faculty about teaching and how best to handle situations with kids." A colleague at the same school echoed the comments, saying, "The administration and other teachers support me in big and small ways . . . and faculty meetings are always about teaching issues."

The six comments about informal support from teachers included four about feeling respected and valued for the talents and skills they brought to the community. One young teacher said, "I feel I have something to give back to my mentor teacher, and that's valuable." A more experienced teacher in a different community said, "The school is interested in my expertise in literature and that makes me feel valuable."

The last question was designed to push the issue of support. We hoped that in asking teachers to think about whether they would choose to stay at the school, they'd consider how fully supported they are in their work. Fourteen of the teachers said they would stay at their school. Six of these spoke of the bright and dedicated teachers with whom they worked, and three talked specifically of the learning opportunities their schools provided. They referred to their ability to start programs or define their own job.

Four teachers were sure they would not stay at these schools. Two of the respondents who answered "No" would not stay specifically because they did not feel valued by their communities.

DISCUSSION OF DATA ON RETENTION

While both the heads of school and directors of diversity spoke highly of orientation programs, teachers did not mention them as particularly supportive. Where heads and directors of diversity agreed that orientation was a critical piece simplifying the early weeks of school, teachers cited ongoing support as the most critical component of their work.

The types of support mentioned by teachers of color are those that any faculty member needs in order to be comfortable and challenged in the workplace. Formal mentoring programs are only as good as the people mentoring and the time allotted to the task. Teachers of color spoke most passionately about a school culture that valued individuals for the skills and talents they contributed to the community.

All three groups agreed that professional networks of teachers of color outside the school are important, but discrepancies arose over how to use those systems. Teachers of color felt that they needed to know that their schools supported their time and efforts by taking care of their professional needs. Schools need to offer release time and to value the time devoted to external networks.

SOME LESSONS ABOUT RECRUITMENT, RETENTION, AND SUPPORT FOR FACULTY OF COLOR

Heads of School

What do you think needs to happen at this school to retain teachers of color? Generally, is there anything else that you have learned about hiring and keeping teachers of color at your school?

Heads of school were remarkably uniform in their responses to the first question. Seven of the 11 claimed retention issues for faculty of color were the same as for *all* faculty. The syntax and style of some answers seemed to indicate that all people have similar needs in their workplaces. The tone of other answers suggested that individuals' needs were different, requiring schools to design support systems responding to individual needs. The issues the seven heads identified as critical in retaining all faculty members are the following:

- pay and benefits, especially tuition remission for teachers' children
- opportunities for professional development, particularly support for graduate study

- support of individual needs for professional growth (this presupposes knowing the faculty well enough to know what types of professional growth are appropriate)
- respectful culture in the school community

One head said it with elegance: "We need to develop an integrated professional development program because all teachers need to feel professionally supported, and they all have different needs." Another said, "We must create a community of people who relate and interact with each other on various levels. It is important to promote professional and personal development even when that means the school must be flexible."

Directors of Diversity

What precisely is your job, and how long has the position existed? Have the responsibilities changed since you've been in it? What are the sources of support for your job, the challenges and frustrations? How could your job be redefined at the school to help you be more effective? What needs to happen at the school to retain teachers of color?

The director of diversity job has been defined in many ways with titles as varied as are the responsibilities of the position. Some positions are one-third or one-quarter time, while others are three-quarters to full time with administrative responsibilities. A list of the titles suggests the range of responsibilities.

- Director of institutional diversity
- Director of diversity
- Director of multicultural programs
- Multicultural coordinator
- Coordinator for multicultural affairs
- Mentoring program coordinator

The existence of the position, the person who fills it, and the school's use of the title are subjects of much debate. Three schools had full-time top administrators acting as directors of diversity. (Two were concurrently upper school principals, while one was defined only as a director of diversity.) Three of the schools had experienced teachers coordinating diversity efforts; three had young teachers sorting through the diversity responsibilities, which tended to focus on student support efforts. Only the three full-time top administrators mentioned above had any power to influence hiring decisions.

However their positions were defined, all designated directors of diversity were expected to create and sustain committees to facilitate the discussion of multicultural issues in the school. Almost all were expected to provide support for students of color and their families. Some were expected to recruit students or at least be available for tours for prospective students of color. Likewise, they were expected to talk to candidates of color, even if the directors did not have direct hiring influence. Not surprisingly, when the directors were asked how they would redefine their jobs to be more effective, eight of the nine called for clearer goals. Of the seven responses to the redefinition question, five wanted the school to make the position full time and grant them the authority to move the school forward with realistic and measurable goals.

Those five respondents agreed that the head of school needed to be a driving force behind the process. "The director of diversity should report directly to the head," and, "This needs to be in the head's lap or it won't happen," encapsulate the comments. One respondent was convinced that the position would disappear after he left the next year. He made a distinction between having the head's support and having a head of school who has a vision about diversity issues: "I'm supported by the head, but it's not high on the agenda of the school." Another replied, "I'd like to work more closely with the head. If the head is not directly involved in the thing, it becomes the 14th thing on a list of priorities."

A debate centers on whether a school ought to employ one person to spearhead diversity efforts. Arguments against the position maintain that hiring a director of diversity allows the rest of the faculty to ignore diversity issues. While a school dedicated to diversity hopes all faculty will work and teach with a multicultural attitude, typically a school needs one person to be responsible for progress toward diversity or lack thereof. "Ideally, the director of multicultural programs should be in the position of working him/herself out of a job. If all things are working well, an institution wouldn't need a person asking these questions." While the value of a director of diversity position per se is debatable, if there is no one in a school to constantly remind the community of its goals, diversity will prove elusive.

When asked what schools needed to do to retain faculty of color, the diversity directors had clear and practical suggestions.

- Make teachers of color part of the fabric of the school.
- Design orientations so that teachers unfamiliar with independent schools can understand the culture they are entering.
- Teach young teachers to build boundaries for themselves.
- Create jobs and positions if you find a person you want at the school.
- Create opportunities within the school which will use the breadth of talents available in the community. This may require more frequent rotations of duty.

- Teach the rest of the faculty, especially department chairs, to be aware of the stresses of being a teacher of color in a mostly White school.
- Educate White teachers through anti-bias training.
- Publicize statistics about openings, interviews, and positions filled.
- Develop a clear strategy with benchmarks to measure progress.

Teachers of Color

Are the school's expectations different for you as a faculty member of color than for other faculty members? In what ways? In what ways might the school be more receptive to and supportive of teachers of color who join the faculty?

The first question asked whether teachers of color believed that they were held to different standards than their White colleagues. Eight of 20 responses were resounding "Nos." One young teacher of those eight qualified her response: "No. Except that some people say insensitive, rude things to me, and I'm supposed to just take it."

The remaining 12 teachers replied, "Yes," and described two general categories of ways in which they felt the expectations of their jobs to be different from those of their White colleagues. Eight of these responded that they were expected by teachers, students, and parents to be available to counsel students of color, deliver insightful comments about students of color who were puzzling to their teachers, and generally take on the job of supporting students of color. There were multiple reactions to this expectation. One young teacher said, "It's not a bad thing. I live for this stuff . . . multiculturalism and diversity. But it's time-consuming." Another was clearly tired of the additional expectations: "I'm expected to have greater insight into certain kids. I am not here to teach adults how to deal with minority kids."

Five teachers who felt that the schools held them to different expectations talked about a perceived need to be "better" at their work than their White counterparts. Two said explicitly, "You've got to be good, really good, because they expect that you won't be." Another said, "I feel I must be more than good as a faculty of color." Two other teachers of color expressed similar feelings, but from a slightly different perspective. They thought they were scrutinized more intensely than their White colleagues, making claims of being observed more often and challenged more frequently by parents. Conversely, one teacher spoke of a sense she had that her students and colleagues were sometimes surprised by her success. She thought they held very low expectations for her talents and capacities.

Students made a presentation for Black History Month in one school, and afterward White colleagues congratulated an African American teacher on the work she'd done with the students. "I had nothing to do with that assembly," she said to the interviewer. "It's the assumptions I hate. And they happen every day."

One faculty member commented on the pressure she feels to fit in. She talked about implicit expectations, offering that the differences in expectations were often subtle but ubiquitous. "I'm a different person when I walk into this school. I have to change the way I walk and the way I act. I am from the West Indies and Brooklyn, and I have to leave those parts at the door. They don't want me for all that."

When asked how their schools might be more receptive to new faculty of color, the teachers provided the following list (most items are paraphrased and listed in no particular order of importance):

- work on inclusive curriculum
- hire more people of color
- Recruit more aggressively
- be more honest; direct the dialogue around issues in daily school life
- provide anti-bias and sensitivity training for all faculty
- improve orientation programs for incoming teachers
- recognize difference; don't pamper it

DISCUSSION OF DATA ON RECRUITMENT, RETENTION, AND SUPPORT FOR FACULTY OF COLOR

Again the chorus of comments around clarity seemed most compelling. There is much confusion about how to measure a school's progress toward a more diverse community and how to define an ultimate goal. Only two of the 11 heads could define clear goals. One was guided by his school's mission statement seeking a school community reflective of the surrounding community's demographics. The other's vision invoked a 20-year plan to achieve a faculty of 50% teachers of color in all levels of the school. The other nine heads were more oblique.

Underneath all the confusion lie more difficult questions. Why do schools want to be more diverse? How diverse do schools want to be? In order to generate any real momentum toward diversity, schools need to be clear about the extent of their commitment to diversity and what that commitment means in terms of action. They must express the ways a diverse community fits into the educational mission of the school. These decisions must involve the board and the administration.

The study shows that directors of diversity want to understand their roles and that schools should design the position to fit their culture and needs. Then, schools should take care to find a person who brings appropriate skills to that position. Too often schools find the most inexperienced person of color in the school to assume additional duties and are disappointed when their vague sense of what the job should be is not accomplished. Schools need to be precise about what is expected from the director of diversity and what training is appropriate for the position. They must specify the types of support that will be given to the person who fills the role. If schools are serious about wanting to hire and retain faculty of color, they ought to empower their diversity coordinators to influence hiring decisions.

The board of trustees and administration need to set policy and establish benchmarks that clarify what diversity means for the school and how the community will know when it gets there. Directors of diversity need a clear mission if they are to help move the school forward. Most feel they should report directly to the head. Because the head uses the mission of the school to guide the school's journey, leadership on diversity issues needs the power and scope of the head to touch every aspect of school life.

EMERGING THEMES: CONCLUSIONS FROM THE INTERVIEWS

Philip Kassen, Mark McLaughlin, Doug Norry,
Michael Simmonds, and John Yoo

Using the 43 interviews with heads of schools, directors of diversity, and teachers of color in the 11 schools, we sought to identify the broad issues that need to be addressed in recruiting and retaining faculty of color in independent schools. Although we cite directly from the interviews, as independent school teachers ourselves we also brought our own experience of over 20 years of working in independent schools in different states as confirmation of the findings. Five core themes emerged as central considerations in diversifying school faculties.

- the need to define diversity
- importance of commitment
- need for support and leadership
- call for open communication
- significance of a critical mass

Defining Diversity

Defining diversity in independent schools seems nearly as difficult as achieving it. Interviews with independent school personnel yielded a wide range of perspectives on this subject. Opinions varied across schools as well as among members of the same institution.

One faculty member questioned the degree to which schools actually were achieving diversity when they selected faculty of color from the so-called "right" universities. By recruiting only from "elite" institutions, such as Yale, Harvard, and Brown, schools conform to the interests of majority parents, who desire "insulation" from "real diversity." Parents tolerate the presence of faculty of color, this teacher asserted, "as long as we went to the right schools and we 'look' like them."

Differences of opinion existed as to which races, ethnicities, and cultures should be considered "of color." An example of one point of view came from a head of school, who stated, "When I think of people of color, I usually tend to think of African Americans—that to me seems the most important group of people for us to get to know." He justified his belief by asserting that he was not sure whether non-African American faculty of color "even considered themselves of color."

There is confusion about whether issues for individuals of different ethnicities and races are the same. An Asian American teacher said, "I am concerned that people lump all of the different groups together." This teacher expressed concern about the dominance of African American influence in diversity efforts, particularly in reference to the People of Color Conference. When she attended, she said, "many of the issues did not pertain to me . . . the conference was geared to African Americans. I don't think I will go back." One director of student diversity acknowledged divisions among nonmajority faculty at his school. He, perhaps unintentionally, identified the source of this dissonance when he asserted that women and Asian American faculty at his school "may have a problem with the fact that two Black men run the diversity office."

Others suggested that attempts to diversify should account for factors such as the international composition of a school's student body and should include not only a commitment to diversity of races but concern for diversity in terms of open discussion of sexual identity. Perhaps the best articulation of what schools should attempt to achieve came from a fourth-grade teacher. She stressed the need for diversity of all kinds—of race, of culture, of background, and of socioeconomic class. Schools invite trouble when they attempt to "fill places . . . with blanket labels." Instead, they need to "recognize that individuals come with their own baggage" and "should not expect everyone to fit into the school in the same way." Schools will be richer places when they are able to go beyond tolerance, when they are able to "accept and embrace . . . differences" within their communities.

Issues relating to student diversity centered on the need for schools to encourage greater sensitivity and awareness among majority students. White students who "make disparaging comments to other students" ought to be made to see the painful nature of their words. There must be sensitivity, as well, to the concerns of students of color "who feel social problems with the other students who often are more affluent." This extends to teachers as well. One faculty member asserted that "it is very difficult to teach at a school where the student population comes from such a different world." One head suggested that diversity directors could serve as the vital link between students and faculty of color and the majority populations of the schools. A director of student diversity cautioned that merely creating an administrative post to deal with diversity issues would not, by itself, result in a supportive school culture. The challenge in creating change is great in schools where the "student population . . . is conservative," and "the students of color either feel apathetic or powerless, so they are not helping the situation."

Commitment

Commitment to creating a diverse and accepting community is an essential component in creating effective efforts to increase the recruitment and retention of teachers of color. This commitment must be reflected by the mission of the school and embodied in the words and actions of the head and board of trustees. The community as a whole must trust that the leaders of the school are following the stated policies in word and in deed. Several comments indicated that this trust is, in many ways, equally as important as results. As stated by one head, it was important for the school to develop an administrative position to primarily focus on and emphasize the issue of diversification. It has a powerful symbolic meaning because it says to the community, "Someone is keeping watch."

The commitment, or lack thereof, to recruitment and retention of faculty of color is expressed in various ways. One teacher commented that a colleague's "summer program has been great in expanding the applicant pool for [his] and other schools. I think that is great. The fact that they hired me is a sign that they are willing to do something. I am not the type of Black they want to hire. I don't have short hair and the conciliatory attitude." Schools that demonstrate commitment to improving recruitment and retention must not treat "faculty of color as a second thought." Members of one school noted that their school's commitment to diversity was seen in the "multicultural curriculum" and "the school's hiring of teachers of color at job fairs." A teacher commended "the devotion to diversity from the head and the lower school head." She called the commitment "very compelling."

A director of multicultural affairs commented on her experiences with that school's commitment to this effort. The school created a job for her and will do so for talented teachers of color in order to increase the diversity of the faculty. Her school's commitment is manifested in the fact that the school has had a position similar to hers for 10 years. This school's commitment to diversity has focused primarily on diversifying the student body rather than the administration or faculty. Another teacher at this same school said that the school "does not have a specific policy or guidelines and procedures about hiring faculty of color but rather a statement of commitment. . . . The revised policy for hiring states that there must be a person of color in the applicant pool."

Another school has a similar statement in its faculty handbook. Its head described his school's hiring process: "Every effort must be made to increase the number of candidates of color among candidates interviewed." This school has hosted the annual Diversity Resource Collaborative Teachers of Color Job Fair and has a faculty committee that reviews resumes that come into the school through the Interschool Faculty of Color Job Search Program.[2] There is annual monitoring of the diversity of the job pool. Another faculty member at this school commented, "The maintenance department is all persons of color except for the head of that department, and he is White."

This same school further demonstrated its commitment through its "multicultural assessment plan." This plan, said the head, is used as "a type of screening process to look at the internal environment and culture of the school. Is it a conducive environment?" Approximately 3 years ago the school mapped the entire curriculum in order to determine what types of multicultural items were in the various curriculum areas. The curriculum committee was compelled to determine the authenticity of the school's multicultural curriculum.

Even as schools try to be committed to increasing diversity in their communities, this commitment often is called into question. A frustrated faculty member noted, "Is the school committed to increasing the number of teachers of color? Absolutely not!" He said his job was created during an evaluation year in order to increase the number of teachers of color for that year. His feelings are echoed by a teacher at another school. When asked if the school was committed to increasing and retaining the current number of teachers of color, she replied, "They keep saying it. But I don't see proof. We have good people, but the school is not doing enough."

As one head stated, "The commitment to diversifying faculty needs to come from the top. Faculty of color need to be part of a weave, and the community is hungry and anxious for it. But, if we don't do it thoughtfully— that kind of failure could be detrimental." Once the leadership is committed, the school's actions must be thoughtfully planned. Another added, "A school will have to take some proactive steps to find a suitable applicant base from which to draw, but ultimately it comes down to the fact that all constituents within the school must trust in the vision and the mission with respect to diversity."

Support and Leadership

If people of color are to be retained and accepted into the independent school culture, they must feel supported. Specifically, people of color feel supported by their respective institutions when two fundamental conditions are met: (1) they are provided with professional development opportunities that are consistent with their cultural and professional experiences, and (2) their colleagues "embrace" and "support" their diversity. Not surprisingly, the degree to which faculty of color felt supported in their respective institutions correlated directly with the degree to which institutional leaders were committed to discussing issues of diversity. A head articulated her belief eloquently: "The person who hires someone has a responsibility to that person. People can't just be dropped into a school by parachute. You must attend to issues that are important to people." Some faculty of color expressed the problems faced by heads in addressing the specific needs of people of color. For example, "People of color do not exhibit uniform needs." "Within the group of people of color there are varying needs which would be difficult to address with a singular and specific task."

Nevertheless, some common themes did emerge as being helpful in retaining faculty of color at independent schools. Several people stressed the need to establish "mentoring programs" for new faculty and an "orientation focusing on the specific needs and challenges of faculty of color." This sentiment transcended the normal adjustments that every new faculty member must make in teaching at a new school with respect to all things procedural. "People need someone to talk to . . . not just about teaching and all . . . but about what it's like to be a person of color at one of these schools." In this regard, it seems that people of color may feel supported by other faculty members of color. Other initiatives also were recognized as being helpful in retaining faculty of color. A school sent faculty members to SEED training in California with the goal of initiating in-house workshops for the entire staff. One large school established a monthly "diversity dialogue" in which all faculty members are invited to participate. Antibias sensitivity training workshops provide a similar forum.

A small but vocal faction of faculty of color seemed to resent the need to "sensitize" or "educate" their colleagues with respect to diversity issues. A teacher at one large school articulated his resentment: "I am not here to teach adults how to deal with minority kids. I am not here to run classes for people who are supposed to be teachers. If teachers are open and sensitive, they should be able to teach any kid."

Another important issue that emerged in retaining faculty of color was the manner in which diversity awareness programs were implemented in schools. It is essential not to create an "us" and "them" mentality. Addressing this issue, one head added, my school "has *not* created specific programs for faculty of color primarily due to the general debate which focuses on the concept of treating faculty of color separately and differently—stigmatization versus providing additional assistance to help faculty adapt to a culture which may be unfamiliar." This head may perceive diversity issues as catering to a specific subpopulation of the school.

Ultimately, a discussion about diversity involves a discussion about leadership. They are inextricably connected. Independent schools committed to recruiting and retaining students and faculty of color are led by heads also committed to that goal. It is a top-down priority. A director of diversity expressed this best.

> The school needs to look at diversity throughout the school in terms of curricular issues. There needs to be a person of color in the cabinet of the head of school. People of color need to have a seat at the table where institutional decisions are made. Having a person of color as a participant at the decision-making level would allow the school to avoid fallout from decisions that are made when people of color are missing from the table.

Open Communication

Communication, in the context of these interviews, describes the flow of information—to, from, and within the various constituent groups of the school community. The participants in this process are students, faculty, administrators, trustees, and parents. Those interviewed stated the importance of open channels of communication and the difficulties that have or could have arisen from the absence of such channels. Communication is key, as reflected in the comment of one teacher: "The faculty and administration need to recognize that faculty of color are coming with different experiences." Different perspectives translate into divergent understandings, making open communication an important issue. Another teacher added, "Part of the solution to the problem is that community-wide communication needs to be improved. . . . The health of a community depends on a lot of two-way communication. With little communication, diversification becomes difficult." Further thoughts include:

- "more dialogue—true dialogue—not just scratching the surface"
- "people tend to stereotype without questioning"
- "affirmative action implies that the system was set up to accommodate [you]"
- "we must start with the teachers in dialogue"

Several interviewees stressed the role of the school's leadership in setting an example of creating a safe environment for communication. Responding to this, one head stated, "It is important to allow faculty to 'test the water.' In creating that range, you must be able to respond positively to what people want to do and have a great deal of flexibility of mind in dealing with various requests." But this sentiment does not seem to be shared by his peers. Although no one would argue with the importance of having open communication, many schools experience difficulty in establishing this within their communities. Many teachers spoke about the lack of open communication. One teacher stated, "Key people won't come out and say that this is important." Another added, "The school lacks forums where people can voice their opinions. There were a lot of strained feelings after a recent assembly led by students of color." Lack of open communication leads to miscommunication and incorrect assumptions. This was evident in the comment of one observant teacher: "Too often the school is too complacent, thinking that everything is wonderful." This theme continues in the following comment: "It seems that we probably bring a little bit more to the school than it realizes—maybe a bit too much. If some of these sentiments and different opinions could be understood better by everyone, things would probably be better."

Sentiments have been shared stating that open communication starts with hiring. An upper school teacher noted the following:

> Honesty is crucial. Schools need to be honest about where they are now and what they plan to do in the future. In the hiring process, expectations need to be made clear. If you have expectations about what a person of color will be doing after he or she is hired, those expectations have to be clear from the beginning.

A fourth-grade teacher added, "In the interview or once a teacher of color is hired, the administration should ask questions such as, 'What role will you play as a faculty of color?'" There needs to be a dialogue that leads to a clear understanding and mutual agreement on the role.

Critical Mass

Many independent schools listed the inclusion of faculty of color as a priority in the hiring process. Teachers of color can exert a profound impact on the culture of the school. A director of student diversity observed, "Faculty of color are needed as role models for kids who look like us, are like us." Beyond creating a more comfortable environment for students of color, faculty of color often benefit the entire student body. According to one teacher, "It would be good to have more [teachers of color] for the students. All of the students need to see a more diverse faculty." Data on the ethnicity of faculty and staff at a different school add weight to this statement. While only 9.2% of faculty and 11.1% of administrators are of color, 90.3% of the custodial staff are of color. Seeing these faces every day sends a clear message to the students at this school.

When asked about recruiting and retaining more teachers of color in independent schools, one person responded, "Hire more faculty of color, so we reach a critical mass." It is a simple fact. Recruiting more faculty of color and reaching some critical number will provide a more attractive environment for teaching candidates of color for several reasons.

First of all, hiring more teachers of color will help to alleviate the burden currently felt by existing faculty of color. The teacher who advocated that more teachers of color are important for the students of color, observed that "they could just hire more. Those of us here are overworked in attending meetings on diversity issues; more could spread this work around." In addition to the burden of meetings, there exists a pressure to represent one's race. Another teacher of color expressed relief at the recent hiring of more teachers of color: "I am not the only Black man here. . . . There are just more Blacks, so there is less need for me to always speak up." Contrast this comment with that from another teacher, who stated, "I am expected to know all the answers for students and parents of color."

Related to the issue of feeling burdened, faculty of color at mostly White independent schools find it difficult to escape feeling like a token member of their race. A head recognized this problem: "We will have to hire enough faculty members of color so no one feels like a token. . . . No one should be asked or expected to carry the burden of an entire race on his or her shoulders." Unfortunately, this is happening as schools struggle with recruitment and retention as well as their own policies on this issue. The problem is exacerbated if a school's real racial mix does not meet with its rhetoric. Consider the words of one teacher of color who felt like a "token" after his picture was put in the school's brochure: "It might be different if I was in some all-White New England school—everyone would know I was just some token Negro. It would all be above board. [My school's] rhetoric, however, wants to claim I am the norm and not just a token Negro." Hiring more teachers of color will help to ease this frustration.

A critical mass of teachers of color offers a school much more than a few individual voices. Arguing for more persons of color, a teacher noted that "they would have to build up their support and be prepared to raise consciousness." This issue of raising awareness is important, as discussed by one head: "I have learned that numbers are more critical than curriculum because in numbers there is power. . . . The canon does and will change perpetually with new people and awareness. . . . The power has to shift in real ways before a discussion of cultural and intellectual diversity can be real." Schools need to put teachers of color in positions and then empower them to press for meaningful change.

While few would argue with the logic of "hiring more," what about the notion of a critical mass? There is some indication that hiring more than one faculty member of color in any given year is more successful than hiring only one during a single hiring season. One teacher of color stated that "the hiring of three new faculty of color has made all the difference this year." One head characterized his school's attitude in the following way: "While we have a significant number of faculty members of color, we don't have enough." What defines *enough* faculty members of color? A critical mass will be achieved when there are enough faculty of color so that none feels the burden of representing his or her race; none feels like a token. Moreover, there need to be enough faculty of color to bring important issues to the table. Finally, one teacher described his school this way: "It is a pretty diverse place. There are enough different people here to create an interesting dialogue."

While it might not lead schools to one definite number, a discussion of the notion of "enough" seems like a good place to start because it would lead a school to have a specific goal and be held accountable to reaching that goal. Obviously, the number will depend on the overall size of the school and should not be suggested as a ceiling. Teachers and administrators of color should be included in the dialogue of how many are enough. This will help foster communication within independent schools.

CONCLUSION

Clearly, there is wide agreement about the need to improve the recruitment and retention of teachers of color in independent schools, as well as wide agreement about the difficulty of the task. There is much disagreement, however, regarding specific goals and procedures. It is apparent that there is no one answer or process that will work for all schools. There are, however, questions that all schools can ask themselves in order to address the five themes identified in this report.

DEFINING DIVERSITY
- Who is included in the definition of a diverse faculty/administration/board?
- How does the school deal with the question of assimilation?

COMMITMENT
- What does the mission statement say about diversity?
- Does this statement accurately reflect the needs and desires of the current school community?
- Is the school's commitment to improved recruitment and retention of faculty of color demonstrated in ways that are visible to, and understood by, the community?
- Is this demonstration visible externally (recruitment) and internally (retention)?
- Does the community trust that the head/school community are doing what they say they are doing?

SUPPORT AND LEADERSHIP
- Is the leadership of the school involved in the process of improving recruitment and retention of faculty of color?
- Is this leadership clear, thoughtful, open, and honest?
- Is there a support structure for all teachers, in general, and for teachers of color, in particular?
- Are faculty of color embraced and supported by colleagues and offered professional development opportunities consistent with their culture?
- Are there programs to increase the level of tolerance and understanding among White faculty and families?

OPEN COMMUNICATION
- Does information flow from the head and administration to the entire faculty and vice versa?
- Does the school market its commitment to diversity, as a priority, both internally and externally?
- Are the head/administration approachable?

CRITICAL MASS
- Has the community set goals for itself in terms of the minimum number of faculty members, administrators, and board members of color needed?
- How is this number set and who is responsible?

The process of seeking answers to these questions is important, if not required, for independent schools, which must reflect the changes occurring in society at large. This includes having more diverse student bodies and faculties. Although specific results from decisions and plans that emerge from grappling with these questions will vary, the process certainly will yield important improvements in schools and, thereby, in communities.

Should I Stay or Should I Go Now?

Lisa Arrastia

Francis W. Parker School, IL

It is the 1970s. I am growing up uptown, in Harlem, in New York, in a predominantly African American community, yet I spend my school days downtown, in an all-White independent school. Sending me to the Lenox School is my parents' attempt to save me from the miseducation that is taking place in the public schools in our neighborhood. They have no idea of the precarious situation in which they have placed me. I become instantly bicultural, a girl who lives between two worlds and learns the language and secrets of both.

Diane Jurgenson's (fictitious name) mother is brushing her hair. The two of them seem like princesses to me, their hair so blonde and thick. With every stroke a sheaf of it slaps softly across the upper flat of Diane's back. The continuous sound is almost meditative. And I ask naively: "Diane, I always stay over your house. How about next weekend you come over to my house?" And then Diane attempts to respond: "That would be greaaa . . ." And then there is a slight tug. The mane yanked to draw attention. Mrs. Jurgenson with her left hand, right hand still holding a tress of flaxen locks, pats my thigh and says: "Nothing against you, dear Lisa, but I would never let MY daughter go UP there where THOSE people live." I nod equivocally, conditioned in school to accede in the face of statements like this from people who look like Mrs. Jurgenson.

    I get on the bus and march my little sixth-grade frame up into the face of my mother, a feat to be attempted only once in a lifetime, and I state like a malapert, "How dare you let us live UP here where THOSE people live? Diane Jurgenson's mother wouldn't do that!" Suddenly my cheek is stinging, and after, Mommy says, "Fool, you ARE those people!"

At age 18, after surviving 12 years of a culturally complex and socially confusing independent school education, I decide to declare quietly to myself: I AM AN AFRO-CUBAN AMERICAN WOMAN. Naming this identity is important to me, because until now it has meant only shame. My tenacious adolescent attempts to hide behind the veil W. E. B. Du Bois described in 1903 are weakening. It is not until 80 years after Du Bois's psychosocial revelation that this thin layer of protection and denial is challenged.

*I am sitting in James Baldwin's History of the Civil Rights Movement
class at the University of Massachusetts at Amherst. Baldwin's first
words are: "Whiteness is a concept." Five minutes into the class my veil is
lifted and I peak out, immediately understanding, on an intellectual and
emotional level, the sociohistorical implications of my ethnic identity
and therefore my shame around it. On that day, in the presence of one
of the most prophetic minds in the United States, I realize that I must
find something that I have been missing: My self.*

I am no longer a Lenox School girl. I don't do what is expected or appropriate, not that I ever really had. The teachers had implied "Quiet!" at lunchtime by tapping me lightly on the shoulder when I laughed loudly at something
funny; and they had insinuated "Hush now!" by catching my eye and bringing their pale index fingers slowly to their puckered lips when, at boys' basketball games, I cheered the way the men did in my family on Monday nights.
I never *really* internalized this particular tacit Lenox rule. No matter how much
I wanted to, I was never ever *really* able to master the sort of complaisance
that this polite society implicitly required and requested for its proper functioning. And so often, because the messages about these sorts of cultural rules
were unspoken, I ended up feeling unsuited, inappropriate, improper, and
unbefitting of the kind of academic and social atmosphere of which I was being
granted the privilege to partake. At home, at my table, there were always
immense reverberations from clamorous, almost euphonic concurrent talk;
there was always brilliant, tumultuous laughter over the deliberate pum-pum
of Señor Candido's congas and cigar smoke that swirled around grandma's
wide hips as she spooned *mas platanos* onto my plate already filled with
yellow rice y *frijoles negros y carne asada y* . . . but, like every other student at Lenox who existed within that socially and culturally controlled environment, I *tried* to conform to their standards. I *tried* to be contained and
cultivated and cultured and refined. I tried to become civilized.

*But tonight, tonight I will make loud noises with my wide mouth like we
do uptown. I will dance hard, and swing my big Black ass to the bump
of funky beats. This resolve makes it certain that I will never return to
Lenox to visit or reunite or donate. And it becomes certain that I will
stop my pathetic efforts to do the culturally impossible: I will no longer
modify manner or voice or dress or language or hair. Nor will I exchange ritual, and what is familiar and feels right, for the hope of a
success based on someone else's cultural values.*

It is the summer of 1996. I collect my belongings, my experiences facilitating diversity and conflict resolution workshops and programs in New York's

rural and urban public schools, and I move to northern California. I leave family, best friends, the familiarity of heat and humidity turning soon into cold and frost. Now, after 13 years I am going back to an independent school, but this time as an administrator, as a teacher. Before I accept the job as director of diversity and English teacher at Marin Academy, I work hard to rid myself of the inner voice that keeps repeating: You should continue to work with your people in communities where low-income kids and students of color are denied access to the basic necessities of a decent education. And what if independent school is still the same polite society where appropriateness is determined by artificial cultural standards dictated by one dominant culture and founded on a false notion of excellence, virtuosity, and superiority?

Once I successfully expunge the voice, I am able to say *Yes*—yes to access, privilege, professional ease, support, comfort, beauty, and relatively unbureaucratized educational creativity. Maybe, I hope, it will be different. Maybe the nature of independent school has changed. Maybe the environment will not lure me in with its false promise of social acceptance in the dominant culture. Maybe I will not feel so compelled, so obligated, so coerced into the forfeiture of self and identity. Maybe *I* have changed, I hope.

An incorrigibly dry but hot August in California. It is just a few weeks before my third year begins at Marin Academy, and I am thinking: Just 4 years ago I was one of those people walking the halls of those academic prisons masking as public schools in the South Bronx and Bushwick Brooklyn. Four years ago I was carrying a roll of borrowed toilet paper on a hanger to a bathroom with no doors; I was toting markers and construction paper from the trunk of my car, bought with my own money; and I was struggling to avoid the temptation to deliver programmed and virtually automated lessons "on" diversity and "on" conflict resolution in an environment that unconsciously created the justification for violence and that honored the mechanical and the divisive.

And now, 4 years later, so quickly, I am working without the worry of an approaching winter with broken school radiators or of brushing biting ants, indoors, off the neck of a screaming third-grade boy. And within this delight, I hate myself, but like a good little independent school girl, I deny the loathing, which is really condemnation and reproof, and I return to this privilege I have chosen to accept. So, within this Africa-like heat, I make iced tea, I sit in front of my school-provided G3 laptop, and I fall willingly and joyously into planning creative educational moments for my willing and oh-so-able and prepared, predominantly White wealthy students . . . all along knowing that as I suck on cool cubes of ice there are teachers carrying toilet paper on hangers to bathrooms with no doors.

Time passes and somehow (and I know I know how) I am a teacher of color who suffers from privileged liberal guilt—a guilt that is ironically mixed with a sense of entitlement. I catch myself feeling guilty for working in an environment like Marin Academy.

Although my teaching remains, in Hooksian terms, a subversive act—because the core of it revolves around deconstructing the very environment in which I teach and in which the students learn—I see that I have in some ways acceded to the overwhelming cultural ecology of the place. I choose my cultural battles, which ones I will fight and when and if. However, the lines defining what is personal, political, or professional are often nebulous. I am always of color here, and then sometimes a teacher, an administrator, or an adult with multiple identities. I am always Black in this place, because Whiteness is so much everything that it is both all things and nothing at all, and so I am obvious, noticeable, highlighted against an unnamed background.

And yet I remain entitled, professionally, anyway, despite the *independent* school dilemmas of wearing an ethnic identity. It is true that I am an *independent* school teacher. But there is a certain cognitive dissonance for me based on the benefits that this status holds and the disaffirmance and discrediting of my position as a teacher and senior administrator of color by some of the adults and students in the community.

Me: *Good morning!*
Them: *Don't you think you might need a late slip this morning, LaKwonda?*
Me: *Oh, I'm not LaKwonda. She's a student. I'm a teacher here.*
Them: *Oh, I am sooo sorry.*
Me: *No problem. That's okay.*

Me: *Your daughters and sons are learning to connect seemingly disparate societal issues while learning the basics of grammar, syntax, and oration.*
Them: *You are so articulate. Where did you get that vocabulary?*
Me: *School?*

Me: *A segment of this class will focus on youth identity and how it is represented in literature and film.*
Them: *I didn't know I was signing up for a "P.C." course.*
Me: *What does "P.C." mean?*
Them: *It means I didn't know that I was gonna, like, have to learn about racial stuff.*
Me: *Huh?*

Me: *Using predominantly female authors, this class will focus on British literature within the historical context of British imperialism.*

Them: *I didn't know I was signing up for a "P.C." course.*

Me: *What does "P.C." mean?*

Them: *It means I didn't know that I was gonna, like, have to learn about racial stuff.*

Me: *Huh?*

Me: *Why don't we meet in my office to discuss . . .*

Them: *Why do* you *get your own room?*

Me: *Well, I teach and perform my other function as an administrator, so I guess they thought keeping it all in one place would be easier.*

Them: *I don't get my own space.*

Me: *I'm sorry.*

Them: *Why do* you *get your own printer?*

Them: *Why don't* you *have to chaperone a dance?*

Them: *Why do* you *get to meet with the administrators regularly?*

Me: *Because I am one.*

The incredulity with which this mixture of inquiries and assertions comes, is what is most galling. And it is almost impossible for me not to take all of this personally. Unlike the positions of business manager or external affairs director, mine remains closely related to who I am and what I believe. And this may be one of the ultimate dilemmas of being a teacher and administrator of color at an independent school: What we do often becomes mixed with who we are.

It is the spring of 1998. Hiring season in independent schools, and I ask myself the same series of questions I have asked of myself each year at this time: Should I stay or should I go now? If I stay, will I recover? Have I lost myself again? Would I even know if this has happened already? I keep hoping that I have not actually succumbed to polite society. Professional entitlement is beguiling and enticing, and it is so easy to fall in, to become a part of, to become a curmudgeon who complains about both the small and the big in the same breath, and more important, because of some of my comforts here at Marin Academy, it can be so easy for me to forget why I am here at all.

I am frequently susceptible to being annoyed by little things here. For example, I get slightly piqued when I arrive at school in the morning and each adult I encounter on campus wants to chat or say, "Good morning," before I have had my coffee. Or when it is raining and I have to walk from Founders Hall to the Administration building with my papers up under my jacket. Or when I have to use the official crosswalk on Mission Avenue when my destination is the Fine Arts Center situated directly across the street, directly across from my office. Or when I have to open the iMac or multimedia lab for other teachers' students. Or when I have exactly 5 minutes to reconnect the wires on the projector in the lecture hall so that my class can watch a movie with THX surround sound. Or when it takes maintenance an entire day to come down and clean the Pepsi stain from my carpet or when the academic office schedules 15 students into one of my English classes when I have enough matching cushioned swivel chairs for only 13. Oh, the woes of working at Marin Academy.

And then I think of Balboa High School, a severely underfunded public high school of about 1,000 Latino, Southeast Asian, and Black students located in the Excelsior district of San Francisco. This is the place that inspired a courageous and formidable Balboa teacher, Shane Safir, and me to co-design a collaborative project involving my honors level English literature class at Marin Academy and Balboa's U.S. History class. Marin Academy and Balboa, two schools from very disparate academic, ethnic, and economic environments, engaged in a reflective and action-oriented study of broad conceptual educational issues, societal messages about youth, school funding, affirmative action, and California education law. The project was so successful that it became the focus of an hour-long KQED public television documentary entitled *Making the Grade*. Many aspects of the project were moving, memorable, awesome, and life-changing. It was when I took my 18 students to shadow Shane's 52 that I was reminded of who I had become as an adult professional member of an independent school, or perhaps I should say, what I had returned to being.

I was annoyed when we first entered the building and the security guard neglected to say, "Welcome," and instead demanded rudely that Aaron Wilde (fictitious name) remove his baseball cap. I was annoyed when the student I shadowed, knowing that we were already 10 minutes late for her first-period class, Spanish I, took her time negotiating the two bridgeways, four hallways, and three flights of stairs that we had to travel. When we finally arrived almost 20 minutes late, the teacher barely responded. On this day, 5 months into the school year, 25 students were crammed into decrepit wooden desks learning how to count to 15 in Spanish. Kids' heads were down on their desks, while others were reading horoscopes in the *San Francisco Chronicle*; still others chatted noisily as the absurdly simplistic lesson droned on.

It's hard to describe. Everything there—the ramshackle conditions, the dearth of supplies, the byzantine bureaucracy, the very air—seemed in league to beat those folks down. Adults and kids. Weird, but it seemed impossible to breathe. I immediately left my annoyance at the door, tip-toed to the back of the room, squeezed myself into a desk and within 20 minutes understood how easy it is to become hopeless in the face of scarcity and ineptitude. Balboa, a public educational institution, offers few academic opportunities for its students, and yet Marin Academy and Balboa students compete neck and neck for admission into the same colleges. By their senior years, students at Marin Academy inevitably will have taken at least 3 years of honors classes and chosen from no fewer than 13 advanced placement (AP) courses. A Balboa student, if not placed in the right academic track in freshman year, might be allowed to take only one of the two AP classes the school offers.

I am entitled at Marin Academy. Each day, I claim a right to easy access to copiers, parking spaces, small class sizes, multimedia labs, and laptops. I neglect to remember that they are simply privileges I am granted because I made a choice to teach here. I made that choice because I was able to, and after a day at Balboa I was reminded how many kids there are in this country who have few if any choices about school, neighborhood, or income.

Since my work with Balboa, I have decided not only to be conscious of my privilege, my entitlement, and my choice to stay at Marin Academy, but to make sure that I actively resist that which makes it okay for me to have so much and so many to have so little.

It is the year 2000. It is my fifth year on the inside and yet the question returns: Should I stay or should I go now? Am I not the Black Cuban who supposedly is committed to those large concepts that are encased in two small words: "equity" and "justice"? And here I am, still in the place to which I swore, at age 18, that I would never return? Why am I still at an independent school? And these are the more personal questions, are they not? Is not the larger, more significant global question: Can The Work be done here, in places like this? My answer: I don't know. I am just not sure.

What I do know is that at Marin Academy I can selfishly revel in teach-ing. Here, at an independent school, I can consistently combine my best ef-forts to teach the basics—personal and persuasive essay writing, grammar and vocabulary, presentation, practice in oration and rhetoric, and scholarly re-search—with participatory, organic student and teacher learning. Here my students and I conduct historical, literary, and sociological studies. Our stud-ies range from the rights of youth and the U.S. Constitution to the social con-struction of race and equity in education. I am able to teach the basics while simultaneously exposing students to socially relevant content.

In each class meeting, as the kids discover new ways to look at old is-sues inspired by our readings and class discussions, I must either relearn something I thought I knew well, or research that which I never knew before. In many ways, the students have stepped outside of the academic and social confines of the room and the campus. With my guidance and some of my expertise, *the students* determine the information they need to know in order to conduct their studies. Consequently, more and more, they express a need to use the outside community as a resource for contextual understanding. My students crave knowledge, search for it themselves, and feel about their education—as Adrienne Rich states about writing—as if their life depended on it. The result has been the development of a learning environment and teaching experience that is dynamic, exhausting, and exciting. Students are engaged in their own learning and passionate about issues that are greater than themselves, and they now ask to know the basics because they want to present intelligently what they have learned. The students realize that it is important for them to be responsible to the society in which they live.

But is this because of me and what *I* am committed to in terms of education, or is this because of the overarching mission of independent schools and the kind of teaching and learning environment that they are able to provide? And isn't this what I wanted and why I wanted to do this thing called teaching? Didn't my childhood experiences in independent school, inside polite society, inspire in me a personal and professional obligation to help kids wrestle with the tangled complexities of self, other, and difference? Yet all of this professional, and in some ways sociopolitical, fulfillment has occurred where many of the students probably would survive life with or without my help as a teacher or an advocate, because almost all of them, at least 87%, are already socioeconomically advantaged. And so, in remembering this fact, I am once again faced with that question that challenges me to choose this place—an independent school—or go back.

It is a warm fall. The heat is reminiscent of the day I gave up what I thought I knew in terms of teaching. I am trying to figure it all out—me, those 12 years, and now 5 more years on the inside of this place of independence. Like history is, it is all so confounded and twisted, so personally delicate and yet also so clear and straightforward, and it is not really history, not yet anyway. I am still here, Black inside an independent school environment that allows me to be a creative educator and yet brings back the oldest ache I know.

The neighbor's daughter raises her voice to a shrill pitch as I am writing this. She is running from something that is not really dangerous. It is the sound of her play that reassures me that teaching, wherever I do it, is a good thing. Right now nothing stands between this child and freedom, and right now, like me, she is loud, impolite, and has a decision to make. Should I stay or should I run now?

How Did I End Up Here?

Erik Resurreccion

The Allen-Stevenson School, NY

I often ask myself that question, "How did I end up here?" with regard to teaching in an independent school, as well as the natural follow-up question, "What am I *still* doing here?" I decided to become a teacher as a sophomore at Dartmouth College after taking an education course that opened up the world of teaching as a possible career path for me. The declining state of our nation's schools drew my interest. I felt compelled to make some contribution to the struggle to improve them.

I imagined myself returning to New York City, where I attended public elementary and junior high schools before entering a public high school in Manhattan. I knew the dire conditions this system faced and felt it was my duty to return and serve these schools. As a person of color, I was energized by the idea of serving the diverse populations of the New York City public schools, particularly since these children do not always have the opportunity to be taught by caring, committed teachers and often do not have the latitude to choose the schools they want to attend.

Yet, in my 9-year teaching career, I have taught primarily in independent schools. I am currently a second-grade teacher in a private all-boys school on the Upper East Side of Manhattan. This is my third independent school experience. What explains this, given my commitment to public education and my desire to give back to my community?

When I graduated from college, I knew I was not yet prepared to enter a public school classroom. That would not be fair to my students. I still had much to learn and wanted to get teaching experience under my belt before I made that leap. My college professors advised me to become an assistant teacher in an independent school. After registering with a couple of independent school placement agencies, I was offered a job as an assistant in a first-grade class at a Quaker school in the Philadelphia area, where I worked for 2 years.

I enrolled in a graduate school program in elementary education in New York City and was placed in an internship program in a public school for the first half of the year and then in an independent school for the balance of the year. I had an incredible experience in the public school and it reaffirmed my

109

original desire to be a teacher. However, since I had completed the required internship but I had not finished all the necessary courses for my degree, I sought another position as an assistant teacher. I knew that as a lead teacher, I would devote a great deal of time and energy to my professional responsibilities both inside and outside of the classroom. I felt that if I took a lead job while still in graduate school, either my classroom or my studies would suffer. Not wanting to make that trade-off, I decided to seek an assistant teaching position once again.

While in graduate school, I returned to independent school teaching, mainly because independent schools are the only institutions that offer assistant or associate teaching positions, which was as much responsibility as I felt I could handle. Teaching in a private school would be only temporary, I thought. Once I finished my degree, I planned to seek a job in the public school system. As it turned out, that did not happen.

As part of my studies, I decided to research and write a thesis on faculty of color in independent schools. This project, which began as a way to fulfill a degree requirement, became a personal journey. I had never expected to be teaching in independent schools. But for several compelling reasons, I found myself attracted to independent schools. I want to be available as a mentor and role model for students of color so that they feel they have a faculty member whom they can approach and who will be their advocate. I also want to be there for the White students. It is important for White students to see a person of color in a position of authority. By being in a school and by getting to know students well, I can play a part in combating racial stereotypes.

I feel a strong sense of responsibility to represent the voices of people of color. I often wonder, if I were not there, who would make sure racial issues are continually discussed in an appropriate way? Who would be there to counter the assumptions often made about students and families of color? This is no indication of a lack of commitment to eliminate racism on the part of my school's administration. I have a strong and active presence in the school. Whenever racial issues arise, even if I am not part of the conversation, the school is likely to consider my perspective in dealing with issues of diversity. They know that if they do not, I will surely communicate my thoughts. I am the school's racial conscience. My administrators and colleagues often seek me out as a sounding board and as a consultant in problem-solving issues concerning diversity.

In addition to the pressure I place on myself to be a role model and advocate for issues concerning diversity, my school, similar to other independent schools, adds pressure by asking us to take on many of these responsibilities in a formal way. This role is a burden. While at first I was flattered to be asked to fulfill what I considered an extremely important role, I also felt that, in a sense, the administration was taking advantage of me and my idealism. Taking on these additional responsibilities adds stress to the job, and generally faculty of color are asked to do so without being compensated. Are all other teachers taking on duties in addition to the many demands of being a teacher? I need to be a liaison to families. I need to help in educating the faculty. I need to be available to the students. I need to be the racial conscience for the White faculty and administration.

I have seen so many teachers and faculty of color suffer burnout. And we also just get tired of always having to be the voice for racial issues. I have seen people take on the position of diversity coordinator, but then they are given no power and no budget. They just have an advisory role and the advice always seems to be brushed aside by the administration in their schools. They make suggestions to move forward on issues but the suggestions are rarely taken seriously or acted upon. It appears that often the diversity coordinator position exists so a school can say they are doing something about diversity. But faculty of color feel used when, in reality, nothing changes. That is something I want to avoid, and because of what I know happens in other schools, I am always cautious when I hear about a diversity coordinator position available at another school. It sounds like an administrative position but often results in reducing a teacher's effectiveness.

There is another disconcerting fact about being a teacher of color in an independent school. We are treated as replaceable parts in the independent school system. I have seen colleagues in other schools who have taken similar roles and responsibilities as I describe I have taken in my own school. Ultimately, they have become frustrated at the lack of change within their institutions. And when these faculty of color move on, the school always seems able to get someone new, fresh out of college, who does not know the history of the school's dealings with issues of diversity. These new teachers and faculty of color, with their fresh energy, often go through the same cycles of delusion and hit the same roadblocks. They get frustrated and leave, and the cycle is repeated. There does not seem to be a real commitment to change on the part of many schools.

Part of the problem is that independent schools tend to believe in the "silver bullet theory." Faculty and administrators in schools claim they had a workshop a couple of years ago and devoted a series of faculty meetings to issues of diversity. A "been there done that" attitude pervades some independent schools that have been exposed to the issues of diversity without substantial follow-up and action steps. Making significant progress in diversifying schools requires a great deal of courage and commitment to drastically change the culture of the school, and hard work to sustain it.

How do I continue on? The only way I have found to decrease the pressures I feel working in an independent school is through the support networks

I have developed over the years. The biggest contribution to my support has been my attendance at the NAIS People of Color Conference that is held annually for teachers, staff, parents, and students in the independent school community. Through my participation in these conferences, I have developed friendships and a network of professional connections, and have received an affirmation of my work, knowing that there are others struggling and dealing with the same issues.

I remember the first time I attended a conference. I was amazed and energized by being among hundreds of brown faces, all of whom were working in independent schools. That made a powerful impression on me. I was not alone, and through listening to others tell their stories, I began to feel empowered to express my thoughts and feelings about working in independent schools. The conference felt like a true celebration of the wide range of cultures and ethnicities present. Instead of having to mask my ethnicity in the independent school setting so that I could fit in or make myself palatable to the community, I could be myself. For the first time, I felt proud to be a person of color working in an independent school.

Because of this first experience, I feel it is necessary for me to keep returning to this conference year after year. I reconnect with old acquaintances, have the opportunity to be re-energized, and reaffirm my experiences and presence in an independent school setting. I usually return to my school from these conferences more empowered, and more confident in myself, knowing I am connected to and supported by so many of the others I meet at this conference.

One of the most pressing concerns I have is that there are not enough teachers of color in independent schools. I return to the conference each year to connect with faculty of color who are new to independent schools. If there were a large number of teachers of color in independent schools, the few of us there would be less likely to have to bear the burden of being the lonely voices of people of color. I feel I must do what I can to encourage young teachers of color to stay in independent schools by sharing my experiences with them, and by helping them process the emotions and questions they have.

A once-a-year boost cannot last all year. In addition to the support I receive at the national conference, I have found allies within the schools where I have worked. This has been my other crucial positive experience working in independent schools. I do not feel alone in wanting to create positive change with respect to diversity. It is extremely important to me that others in the school who harbor similar aspirations to change our school culture are NOT just the faculty of color. I am among colleagues who have similar goals and a similar vision of equity and justice for the school.

There are many White administrators, colleagues, and parents who speak passionately about their commitment to diversity in my school. One can hold these pronouncements suspect if there are few other types of conversations one has with them. However, issues of diversity are only one of many common interests I share with my colleagues. I feel connected as a fellow teacher dealing with all the usual demands of the schedule, parents, class preparations, and faculty meetings, and I feel connected to my colleagues as a person with an outside life and interests that are not school related. I feel valued and respected as a member of the school community and not just as a one-dimensional person concerned only with the issue of diversity.

Sadly, I have learned through talking with others that the receptivity to confronting issues of diversity is not happening in many independent schools. Perceptions of where faculty of color can work and be supported, where White faculty, administrators, and trustees are "on board" and looking for ways to work on these issues and move forward, are shared, and general consensus develops as to which schools are the best places to work. Schools may not realize that their employees can be their best representatives or their worst critics. If there is a genuine commitment in a school community to resolve issues of diversity, the information spreads. The end result is that more people of color want to work in these schools. Schools need to honestly decide where they want to be with respect to diversity. Administration, boards, and teachers need to honestly decide how committed they are to diversity.

CHAPTER 5

Three Case Studies: The Wingate School, the Quaker School, and Heights Academy

The research team developed case studies of each of the 11 schools we visited, with the purpose of looking at their work with diversity issues in their faculty. These case studies reported our findings, using our interviews (described in Chapter 4) as their basis. All 11 schools were actively looking at diversity issues, but our interviews and the resulting case studies showed that the schools were operating at various evolutionary stages along the path to establishing a school that is fully representative of America's racial diversity.

From these 11 case studies, we have selected three that best illustrate the varying aspects of those evolutionary stages. These three case studies also illustrate the factors that make the issue of greater faculty diversity so complex. None of our case studies—all done in the diverse city of New York—is typical of faculty diversity in independent schools in the country. Nationally, 47% of independent schools have only one teacher of color or none at all; thus, even the school we call Wingate, which appears to be struggling to attract teachers of color, is doing well by national standards. Nevertheless, the description of challenges and success in these three New York City schools may be instructive for all schools committed to diversifying their faculty. Geographic location matters, but so do visionary leadership, board support, aggressive hiring policies, compensation, mentoring, professional development opportunities, and a receptive school culture.

The Wingate School has a commitment to attracting students of color, but the school has reached a stasis in the number of teachers of color. A new head understands that diversity requires a cultural change in school life, but she is cautious about imposing changes during her first year.

The Quaker School presents a different scenario. Perhaps prompted by a precipitous drop in the number of students and a need to increase enrollment, the Quaker School has succeeded in increasing enrollment by diversifying the student body while simultaneously increasing the number of faculty of color.

Born during the idealism of the 1960s, Heights Academy was founded explicitly to create a diverse community reflecting the dreams of Dr. Martin Luther King, Jr. Through its multicultural curriculum and the diversification of students and faculty from its inception, Heights Academy represents one of the most diverse independent schools in existence.

THE WINGATE SCHOOL

Dennis Bisgaard, Kate Knopp, and Tracy Knox

Wingate is a coeducational, college preparatory day school enrolling more than 1,600 students in grades K–12, with over 900 in grades 7 and up. While Wingate traces its existence back more than 100 years, it has been an independent school for the past 50 years. There are 206 faculty members; 128 are women. Nine faculty members and one administrator are of color; the administrator also teaches. Three of the 100 faculty teaching in grades 7–12 identify themselves as teachers of color. Of 31 board members, one is a person of color. Wingate employs 81 people in maintenance, security, and kitchen staff. Exact numbers of people of color on the staff were not available, but interviewees noted that the staff is predominantly people of color; however, the head of maintenance is a White male.

The first half of Wingate's years of independent school status was as a boys' school, but the school is now fully coeducational. Students of color compose 27% of the total student body in grades 7–12, but less than 9% in the lower grades. Most of the student body comes from Manhattan's Upper East Side, Riverdale, and Westchester. According to two of the faculty we interviewed, there are more Jewish students than any other religious or ethnic group. The faculty are mostly White and non-Jewish. Apparently, the school has a history of a predominantly Jewish board of trustees.

When we visited Wingate, the head of school was in her first year. Everyone with whom we spoke seemed hopeful about her vision and personal commitment to diversifying the faculty. Interviewees suggested a lack of commitment and leadership on faculty diversity before the present head's arrival. Demographic data indicate that the number of teachers of color (4% overall) has remained relatively constant for several years.

There is no written institutional policy addressing the hiring of teachers of color, but the head has personally committed to having at least one candidate of color in the final round for every position. One of the faculty said the new head "is progressive in recruiting teachers of color," but added that Wingate needs to go "off the beaten path to find teachers of color."

When asked if the board of trustees would support her efforts to diversify the faculty, the head speculated that support was not assured. She estimated that while nearly half of the board would be considered truly supportive, a quarter was only tacitly behind her vision and the remainder probably would not support her efforts.

There is, however, a clear commitment from the school to enroll students of color. Wingate is seeking younger children who will remain enrolled through graduation. At the time we visited, the board had guaranteed a 20% increase in funding for scholarships for the next year and another 20% for the subsequent year to help attract and retain students of color.

One faculty member claims that a previous admissions director told his staff to ignore a mandate from the head's office to try to increase enrollment of students of color. The teacher called the former admissions office a "racist hotbed." Wingate recently hired as its new director of admissions a young White woman committed to increasing diversity beginning with the year after our visit. Two school newspapers discussed this appointment as an "indication of significant change" and evidence of the new head's commitment to diversity.

The weekly school newspaper quotes a member of the recent search committee for the director of admissions as saying that although there has been significant change in regard to gender, "there has been no change in diversification in ethnicity. There are plans in place today because [the head] has indicated this as a priority and has concrete strategies in place. I believe that this has been a spoken priority year after year but not one that has been addressed in concrete terms."

Wingate's newly hired head believes the community has suffered from a lack of leadership. She has a vision but acknowledges the time it will take to understand the community enough to move the school toward her vision. She believes a diverse faculty is critical to the school's academic life and marketability.

"Hiring is an art," she says. She expects department chairs to be responsible for recruiting potential hires because department chairs oversee new faculty and have countless interactions with them within their departments. The reality is that department chairs have myriad responsibilities and largely rely on agencies to fill vacant teaching positions.

Four years ago, the faculty created the Valuing Differences Committee in order to foster greater diversity consciousness through special events. The committee comprises mainly faculty members, but administrators and students also attend meetings. The committee plans school-wide activities, such as "Diversity Day," which include guest speakers and special performances. The committee requested that the administration support a full-time director of diversity position, but the administration has remained reluctant. The head, especially, is not convinced that such a position will serve the school, and worries that faculty might feel absolved of responsibility for the issue. She claims the position would allow diversity to be seen as the one person's job rather than as a community commitment. While the committee concedes her point, they argue there is little community commitment without the position; a dedicated "point person" would better hold the community accountable.

Wingate is a highly academic and intellectual community. The principal focus is on individual academic learning, while other social and cultural aspects of school life seem to get less attention. Until this year, there has been no concrete commitment to increasing diversity among the faculty. The lack of change in diversity numbers might be attributable to a group of grade-level administrators at the school who lack initiative and experience about issues of diversity.

Wingate does have an attractive pay scale. Two of the three teachers we interviewed cited salary and benefits as a primary reason for working at the school. Such resources should make recruitment more fruitful. Still, attempts to find faculty of color have not existed in any organized fashion.

According to the head, retaining faculty of color is linked to professional development and support for *all* faculty. There is a mentoring program, but it is not effective. Faculty are not granted additional time to mentor, nor are they trained for the role. Consequently, teachers are left on their own to find support, usually with colleagues in their departments. As such, both personal and professional support is more difficult to cultivate for faculty of color simply because the stresses of the job may manifest themselves differently.

Wingate seems to be on the verge of change. The head is ready to make a commitment to diversity, but a strategic plan and implementation of this commitment have not yet materialized. She is cautious in her approach, concerned that the nature of the commitment and the strategies need to work within, not against, the culture of the school as she is learning it. She understands the rigorous academic and intellectual life of the school as its essence, but hopes to improve its culture and community. There seem to be two realities at Wingate: the talk about diversity on the one hand and the skeletal mechanisms created to support it on the other, which are inadequate to do so successfully. However, the new head's expressed commitment may bring success in garnering the necessary support to effect change.

THE QUAKER SCHOOL

Sidney Bridges, Kathleen Brigham, and Gary Niels

The Quaker School is a K–12 coeducational institution with close to 500 students. There are 88 faculty, of whom 19 are of color. Faculty of color work in every division and hold several administrative positions. The board of trustees has 15 members, including eight Quakers and two persons of color. Most of the Quakers are educators. The first person of color joined the board in 1990. The custodial staff is 50% minority and 50% nonminority. The head of the custodial staff is a Latino.

In the early 1990s, the population of the school nearly doubled, and the percentage of minority students increased significantly. This dramatic change was due largely to the appointment of a new head who was hired to breathe new life into a then-struggling school. The student population is very diverse: 45% African American, 10% Latino, and 4% Asian American.

Although there were some conflicting remarks, we were impressed by the Quaker School's commitment to hiring and retaining faculty of color. The head of school is clearly driving this commitment. He believes that the "demographics of the school should reflect the community in which we live." One of his visions is to have teachers of color in all departments, thus enabling students to have role models in every discipline. To manifest his commitment, the head developed a specific hiring policy in regard to faculty of color: In every search there must be at least one candidate of color as a finalist. He has even expressed a willingness to pay a higher salary to attract more teachers of color to the Quaker School. He believes that remuneration might be a factor in retaining faculty of color. His approach is to "pay them and pat them on the back," while also offering generous tuition remission opportunities for teachers of color with children. The head asserted the need for the school's climate to be receptive and open to its diverse members.

A veteran science teacher of color reinforced some of the head's optimism. She was attracted to the Quaker School as an ideal place for her daughter to attend school. She has noticed a sizable increase in the number of teachers of color at the school since the head arrived 6 years earlier, while also noting that the school culture is supportive and safe for teachers of color. Although she observes that teachers of color are not actively recruited by the school administration, they are naturally attracted to the Quaker School because of its acceptance of all people. This veteran teacher also claimed she did not observe different treatment by the school community toward teachers of color and White teachers at the school: "Everyone is treated the same."

Not all teachers, however, see the school as deeply committed to hiring teachers of color. One assistant teacher complained that she rarely saw teachers of color as candidates. She claimed that other teachers had made her feel awkward and uncomfortable because of her race. Although she has experienced prejudice at the school, she did find a confidant in the upper school principal, a person of color, who simultaneously serves as the director of diversity. According to the teacher, the upper school principal expressed empathy for the assistant's experience and admitted to personally experiencing subtle racist attitudes among some of the upper school faculty.

The head's approach to remuneration for teachers of color was verified by one interviewee who felt that the best way to retain faculty of color would be to provide good benefits such as salary, health care coverage, retirement benefits, and opportunities for professional advancement. Another teacher commented that commitment might be better expressed if the diversity director position was separated from that of the upper school head, creating two positions rather than the present one. The implication was that the director of diversity position has expanded so much that the same person can not simultaneously fulfill both administrative functions at the Quaker School.

The school needs to react vigilantly to both overt and covert expressions of racism among the faculty. One of the teaching assistants we interviewed believed the best way to deal with racism was for the teachers to talk openly, not superficially, about their problems and feelings. From nearly all perspectives, though, the Quaker School seems to be moving in the right direction. The head has a clear vision and genuine commitment to attracting more teachers of color. The school's progressive Quaker beliefs were exemplified in its historical decision to be one of the first independent schools in New York to accept a student of color. This has given the Quaker School a long time to build and foster a climate attractive to and supportive of teachers of color.

In a number of respects, the Quaker School might represent the vanguard of New York City independent school success in hiring and retaining faculty of color. Nineteen of its 88 (22%) full-time faculty members are persons of color, each of whom is characterized by the head of school as being a significant participant in the faculty culture. One is the upper school principal and director of diversity, and another is the head of the technology department. The school's significant faculty diversity and its strong quality (mostly experienced teachers with master's degrees, according to the head) are largely a result of the head's vision and aggressive recruitment policy. The Quaker School advertises widely in a variety of local and national publications, and is tied into several networks.

One of the best indicators of the school's success is what the head describes as its self-generating and nurturing culture. Faculty of color feel comfortable and, as a result, many teaching candidates of color are attracted to the school and those who are hired tend to remain. As one veteran teacher observed, the environment at the Quaker School is open and nurturing. She emphasized the low attrition rate of the school's faculty: People who leave the school leave because they want to pursue other opportunities, not because they are unhappy. Each of the teachers with whom we spoke felt supported by the director of diversity. Nevertheless, the school's efforts to attract and retain faculty of color are not without fault.

Some dissonance exists between the head's assessment of the school's success and that expressed by some of its faculty. Not everyone is aware of the official policy or mission, nor does everyone believe that the school is earnest in the pursuit of its objective. (Clearly, we would need to interview a much larger cross-section of the faculty to substantiate this conclusion. Our sample included two assistant teachers whose feelings of marginalization may have been as much a product of their professional status as their being faculty of color.) Where the veteran teacher painted a virtually ideal picture reminiscent of the head's characterization of a nurturing community, others were far more critical. When asked if the school is committed to increasing the numbers of teachers of color, one assistant teacher replied: "Rumor has it that it is." Similarly, the other assistant teacher queried, "If the school is committed, why is it that most of the candidates whom I see are White?" Each of these teachers also reported feeling isolated, ignored, and often uncomfortable as a result of parent and colleague "standoffishness" and other subtle challenges to their legitimacy. Both were self-conscious of being labeled a "teacher of color" and of being judged on that basis. Despite this, each felt she had the unqualified support of the director of diversity and the firm backing of her faculty mentor.

Despite its difficulties, the Quaker School must be considered a qualified success. Many schools would be satisfied with the Quaker School's numbers, but it is clear that its head is not. Indeed, much of the school's success is attributable to the vision and resourcefulness of its head in fostering change. The school had little diversity when he arrived in 1990, and it is clear that much has occurred since then. The head is invested in the pedagogical merit of having strong role models who reflect the ethnic background of the school's students. He does not appear to be interested in diversity for purely superficial reasons. The composition of the student body is a distinct advantage the school has in fostering a stronger faculty of color presence. Approximately 55% of all students are of color, making the school an even more attractive place to teach for faculty of color. The head has taken advantage of the Quaker belief in the inherent worth of every individual to create a more diverse teaching staff.

A significant struggle the school still faces is its attempt to reach consensus on precisely what constitutes "success" in the recruitment and retention of faculty of color. Despite its numbers, some people feel that not enough is being done. The assistant teachers who mentioned having their integrity questioned raise another impediment: the alienation of other faculty members who perceive that faculty of color receive special treatment. This resentment detracts from the notion that the Quaker School is necessarily a nurturing and positive environment for all faculty of color.

The Quaker School is one of the more diverse in New York and perhaps in the nation, partly because of the diversity of the city and largely due to the efforts and commitment of its administration. Diversity is at the top of the head's agenda, and he has a clear mission for the school's population to reflect its surrounding community. Note, however, that this is a mission created by the head of the school. The Quaker School is on an upswing, experiencing many changes since the new head arrived 7 years ago. Much has been done to draw faculty of color into the school, but more is required. While clearly proud of its accomplishments, the school does not appear to be resting on its laurels. It continues to plan new ways to continue to recruit and retain faculty of color, while creating a school of diverse ideas and cultural backgrounds.

HEIGHTS ACADEMY

Cathleen Randall and Jerry Loewen

Heights Academy is a pre-K–8 coeducational independent day school enrolling 275 students. The student body is approximately 47% White, 30% African American, 20% Hispanic, and 3% Asian. The faculty is approximately 35% people of color.

The Academy's commitment to hiring and retaining faculty of color is strong. It is the current policy of the school to seek a faculty diversity mirroring both its student body and that of the larger community. Unlike the situation with many independent schools, this has been Heights Academy's mission since its inception in the mid-1960s. The school's mission speaks of a "pluralistic society," absent a "predictable majority," in which there is "equal access and equal opportunity" for all. Created during the Civil Rights Movement, the school has been deeply influenced by the vision of Dr. Martin Luther King, Jr. The founding and current head of school envisioned the Academy as a place "to match the dream" of King: an institution of integration and inclusion. The school has received money from the Altman Foundation and the DeWitt Wallace Foundation in its pursuit of multicultural education.

Evidence of Heights' multicultural commitment is not difficult to find. The lack of a White student majority is immediately apparent to visitors. The 35% faculty of color mix is also striking, especially in relation to the faculty of many other independent schools. The board of trustees is similarly diverse.

The curriculum is a shining reflection of multiculturalism and the school's mission to represent as much diversity as possible. The walls are covered with student work illustrating the school's multicultural underpinnings. Faculty and administrators constantly mentioned the school's running conversations, both formal and informal, around issues of diversity, multiculturalism, and the implications of its educational innovations. All participants noted an openness to debate these topics.

Spanish is the only language offered throughout the school; use of the language is not limited to "Spanish classes." Eighty percent of the faculty has participated in the school's exchange program with a sister school in Nicaragua at which a 4- to 6-week language immersion program is offered.

Money is available to faculty members to pursue other professional and personal interests in the summer, with encouragement given to those relating to diversity. One African American sixth-grade history teacher conducted oral history interviews along the Freedom Trail as a means of bringing richer materials to his class and as a way of delving deeper into his personal passion.

The only differences in perception among the people we interviewed concerned the ideal "mix" that the school's diversity should assume. While the suggested number varied, most agreed that more Asian American teachers were needed. The school's administration also hopes to expand its diversity beyond its present state to include more Asian American teachers. Despite an initial gift, Heights was denied a grant renewal by DeWitt Wallace because the foundation believed the school was no longer in need of the money. The head is pursuing other funding to assist faculty of color in the pursuit of higher degrees while still working at Heights Academy.

Perhaps the greatest indication of the Academy's success in recruiting faculty of color is the increasing frequency of unsolicited inquiries from teachers of color who have heard of the school through word-of-mouth. Some present faculty members turned down offers from other schools in the hope of getting an offer from Heights Academy. The school's strong connection with local universities has attracted many intern teachers, who stay on to become "lead teachers." The school's presence at the New York City Job Fair for faculty of color routinely has attracted many other highly qualified candidates.

The school seems to be equally strong in its retention of faculty of color. The head and two teachers described faculty members who left the school: Only one has gone on to teach in another independent school. Others who departed for other teaching positions have gone into public education. Presenting Heights Academy as a "private school with a public mission," the head seeks to train teachers for public school education and reform. While he never wants to lose his best faculty, he sees their departures to public school as another indication of the school's success. The three teachers with whom we spoke seemed content to remain at Heights for the indefinite future. One has been there for 13 years, another for 6, and another was completing her first year.

Many factors can explain the school's success in recruiting and retaining faculty of color. Perhaps being only a lower and middle school makes it easier to recruit faculty, but it is the "culture" of the school, something to which every interviewee alluded, that appears to be a source of motivation and a reason for staying. The rookie teacher defined Heights Academy's view of multiculturalism by noting, "Everyone has a culture." The head encourages teachers to follow personal interests in the classroom and to bring these interests into the curriculum. This personal investment carries over to teachers' treatment of students. Individual cultures, stories, and interests seemed to dominate classrooms. All three teachers were immediately attracted to this "culture," especially in comparison to the environment at other schools. Faculty conversations, formal and informal, constantly push the evolution of the culture. Just as the public definitions of "diversity" and "multiculturalism" continue to evolve, Heights Academy seems to constantly re-evaluate and analyze its actions in light of its goals.

Several other practices related to nurturing and developing faculty appear to support the school's mission. The emphasis on attending professional conferences seems to improve both faculty recruiting and retention. Teachers learn, and the school's name is spread throughout the education community. Within the school, the frequency of faculty meetings (once a week) helps the school anticipate and defuse important issues. One teacher referred to the school's efforts to find challenging jobs within the school for valued faculty members who want to increase their responsibilities. Heights sponsors many in-house workshops, drawing on the expertise of its own faculty and focusing on its own issues. A faculty "Fun Fund" finances everything from telephones and computers to Saturday bowling trips.

Despite having the same head of school for 30 years, the Academy does not seem to have grown complacent or stagnant in any regard. Certainly the issue of multiculturalism continues to attract devoted energy and resources.

As mentioned earlier, the school's biggest struggle seems to center on the appropriate "mix" of diversity for the school. The numerous "right" answers to the problem are bound to create conflict and controversy. We did not see, however, any indications that discussion of this conflict was ever suppressed. In fact, it seemed to be pursued by every member of the faculty and administration.

Another challenge facing the school is its attempt to fund the pursuit of graduate studies by faculty of color. While requests for external grant money for this purpose have been turned down, the head sees continuing education as another means to recruiting and retaining faculty of color. It also addresses the school's larger mission of better preparing all of its teachers for teaching at Heights Academy or in other (public) schools.

CONCLUSION

While the independent school world is making strides in diversifying their student bodies and their faculty and staff, many schools (47%) still have only one or no teachers of color. We chose to highlight the three schools included in this chapter because though they are in different stages of reaching their optimum commitment to diversity each offers lessons for other independent schools. Although the level of commitment to diversity varies at each of these schools, it must be remembered that compared with the national norm these schools are unusually diverse. Even Wingate School, whose commitment to diversity is in its infancy, has nine teachers of color, well beyond the national average. The experiences at Wingate, Quaker, and Heights offer numerous lessons for other independent schools.

The experiences at all three schools indicate that the heads' commitment is highly influential in determining the culture of the school and the climate of openness to faculty of color. For example, at Wingate, the head, who was only in her first year at the school and had yet to formalize policies for attracting and hiring more faculty of color, still inspired a great deal of hope and confidence in the school body and the faculty. Because she—as head and, therefore, in a position of authority—had stressed publicly the importance of hiring more faculty of color, people in the school community could feel confident there would be a palpable change in the future. At Quaker, the head's commitment is clearly a driving force. Teachers are attracted to the school because of the supportive environment for faculty of color cultivated in part by the head. The head has made clear his mission to have the diversity of the faculty and of the student body match the diversity of the community, communicating to others that the school's work is not done. Finally, the head of Heights Academy demonstrates the power of creating and sustaining a mission into which a commitment to diversity has been seamlessly integrated. Most schools cannot match Heights Academy when it comes to their historical commitment to people of color; however, independent schools can learn from Heights' experience and strive to integrate goals for diversity into their mission statements.

The head's and the school's commitment is most obviously seen in the school's approach to hiring. The head of Wingate, while still searching for the best way to ensure that candidates of color are in the hiring process, has hit on a key issue: Clear policy guidelines need to be in place; otherwise, as is happening now at Wingate, things fall to chance. Both Quaker and Heights have the benefit of good reputations that attract faculty of color to apply for jobs in these schools. Quaker's policy of requiring that one candidate of color be included in the final hiring round sends an important symbolic message as well as ensuring that the school works hard to seek out potential candidates.

Interestingly, Wingate and Quaker are both struggling to know what is the best role for a director of diversity. This struggle points to the difficult issue of assigning responsibility for diversity. On the one hand, the director of diversity, especially if given a full-time position, can present noble goals for diversifying the student body, and prevent the faculty and staff from languishing. On the other hand, if this person is in charge, all the other administrators and teachers may feel absolved from actively supporting these goals. Heights offers an edifying example. While there is someone whose sole responsibility is to encourage and support diversity, the head and faculty clearly embrace the school's multiculturalism and take on the responsibility for supporting diversity as well. Also, the school's mission and policies encourage everyone to support diversity.

The diverse student body at both Quaker and Heights also encourages and attracts more teachers of color. It seems clear that a commitment to hiring faculty of color is best paired with a commitment to a diverse student body.

One other interesting point to note about Heights was the level of openness among teachers when discussing the school's strengths *and* weaknesses. Unlike at Quaker, where the head's optimism about the school's commitment to diversity was not echoed by all the teachers, the Heights interviews revealed that the faculty and administration felt comfortable talking about conflicts at the school. Teachers at Quaker expressed a desire to be able to speak openly about conflicts at the school, but that level of trust and confidence did not yet exist at the school.

All three schools—Wingate, Quaker, and Heights—offer insightful examples of how independent schools can strive to attract, hire, and retain faculty of color; however, because of its history and singular success, Heights Academy deserves close attention. If Heights Academy cannot be portrayed as "the answer," it certainly can be used as a "best practice model." Senge's idea of a shared vision, its power, and its influence seemed to be on display.[1] A clear mission begets a clear purpose and a clear product. The fact that this is evident in a school head after 30 years, an administrator of 13 years, a teacher of 6 years, and a novice teacher of just one year speaks loudly to the effectiveness of everyone's efforts.

A few questions remain to be explored. We would like to see the long-term influence Heights Academy has had on its graduates. What high schools do they choose? Do they approach education differently in these institutions? Do they find other schools' lack of diversity troubling? Is the public purpose of the school being realized? Is this a model that would work anywhere, or does it work only because of New York City's diversity and the colleges and universities from which it can draw faculty?

We speculated that the school's "public mission" may account for some of its long-term effectiveness. To focus only on the independent school world limits the extent of one's impact and the possibilities of one's work.

The notion of diversity as a numbers game is evident at Heights Academy only in the sense that a critical number of students of color can attract more students of color and consequently attract more faculty members of color. These critical numbers cannot be reached without significant attention to the cultural diversity evolving in the school. The recognition and celebration of this diversity make all the difference at Heights. It is important to underscore that the school was founded on a mission of a pluralistic community; thus, it has never had to face the hurdle of upsetting the status quo when "numbers" rose over 30%, threatening those long in power. The school seems to value human resources far more than physical resources. Offices were cramped, classroom spaces were carved out, and "coziness" seemed to be par for the course. The attention to people, however, was evident everywhere.

We wonder about the double-edged nature of the head's 30-year tenure at Heights Academy. The vision is definitely not only the head's; the school would not flounder if he were to leave. The fact that the school has not become stagnant after many years under one person's leadership is a wonderful testament to the head's commitment to the ideals on which the school was founded. The stability around this politically charged mission has benefited the school.

Moreover, this mentality at Heights Academy has benefited not just the school, but the larger world of independent schools, which can watch and learn.

The Journey of an Indian American Student and Teacher

Pia Awal

The Dalton School, NY

THE STUDENT

I can still remember my first day of first grade at an independent school. Just like everyone else, I was dressed in my blue tunic and white shirt with a Peter Pan collar. I had my Hello Kitty pencil case and an Eastpack backpack. Like all the others, I was even going to visit a store called P.S. I Love You, after school.

Each of us in our little reading group sat in a separate part of the room. I remember pretending to read the storybook that Miss Wilson had instructed me to read. I pretended because it was boring and I didn't want to read it. I loved reading street signs and highway directions. The simple story line of the books that Miss Wilson gave me didn't compare.

Around 10:00 every morning, a Latina kitchen staff member who was nameless and faceless would bring juice and crackers or cookies into our room. Her existence and identity were never discussed, and we never really questioned. I did, however, wonder why she had to wear a netted shower cap on her head. We would help ourselves to a snack and sit at our desks where we could chat with our friends. One of our favorite pastimes during snack was to draw and in particular to watch our classmate, Laura Hartman, draw. She created realistic pictures of animals, houses, people, and, of course, hearts and rainbows. Laura's handwriting was so precise and teacher-like, that sometimes when Miss Wilson left the room for a few minutes we would have her go up to the blackboard where the schedule for the day was written and change the word *Gym* to *Gum*! Everyone wanted to be able to draw just like Laura.

At lunchtime, we would go down to the cafeteria where we could choose from a variety of foods. While we walked down the aisle following each other, my friends would always comment on what they thought was appetizing and what was gross. On one day when I didn't like the hot lunch, I wanted to eat a peanut butter and jelly sandwich on whole wheat bread. But when I put the whole wheat sandwich on my plate, my friends stuck up their noses and said, "Gross! How can you eat that?" After that day, I always chose to eat white bread in school. It was always easier to choose to eat what most of my friends ate, what they liked, what they approved of as tasty and, of course, cool. Yet I wondered, why did it matter so much what I ate?

After lunch we would go out for recess onto the street in front of our school. Some girls would play with jump ropes; others would just sit and chat, while many of us played with our dolls. It always seemed to me that for some reason the other girls' dolls were better. Were their dolls better because my friends, with their lighter skin tone, looked like their dolls' mommies?

That fall, my sister was born. One morning, my mother came downstairs to put me on the bus. My friends saw my baby sister in her arms from the bus window. Everyone wanted to know her name. When I told some people on my bus that her name was Amrita, they looked at each other and then at me and replied, "What?" My other friends at school didn't understand her name either, and so I decided to stop telling her name. How could I tell them that her name meant nectar of immortality and that she was so special to me, when they couldn't even pronounce her name?

I had a similar problem when I invited friends over to my home. Pictures of Indian gods and goddesses hung on the wall. "Who's that?" they would ask in a curt tone of voice, as if these unfamiliar images were somehow bad, somehow threatening.

My best friend Carrie soon came to express some interest in and acceptance of the little altar in our home. Sometimes we would light candles and place them on the altar. Yet, she repeatedly wouldn't try the Indian food we ate and would sit at the table agreeing to eat only crackers.

Many of my memories of my elementary school seem to end in unanswered questions. One afternoon I came home desperately wanting to know, "Am I Jewish or Christian?" My mother explained that in fact I was neither and that we were Hindu. "But I have to be either Jewish or Christian," I insisted. "My friends told me so."

It was in this system of right and wrong, Black and White, American and, well, something else, that I was initiated to life in America. To my friends, the only categories that existed were the ones they fit into. To my teachers, it seems like their job was simply to teach the academics. It occurs to me that my teachers never considered that I might see things in a different way. My teachers did not seem to respect or acknowledge my experiences. They didn't demonstrate any interest in the winter vacation that I spent in India, whereas the natural curiosity of my peers led to many questions about why I went there and what I did. Nevertheless, I didn't feel like talking, as visiting India still didn't compare with trips to Barbados or Florida.

For me, visiting India was about being with my family in a world where, even if just for 2 weeks, I was not a minority. It was a place and time where

I could talk about food, religion, likes, and dislikes as an individual and to people who just understood.

THE TEACHER

With a bright smile on my face and my portfolio in hand, I would walk into a school as a hopeful young college graduate. Public school job fairs in May and June promised to hold interviews at the end of August. I feared waiting until the last minute. One public school principal in West Harlem shook my hand and offered me a job without even seeing my resume or taking me around the school. The grade I would teach seemed irrelevant to her. The progressive public schools where I had student taught would not think of hiring a recent college graduate, and so I opened my search to independent schools. Some of these independent schools wanted to "mold" their teachers with little prior teaching experience. Other independent schools seemed to pay only lip service to the concept of diversity, as seen in the population that made up the faculty and student body, and in the largely workbook curricula. Memories of my own childhood would flash before me.

Yet, entering the small, cozy schoolhouse on the Upper East Side of Manhattan, I was warmly greeted by the African American lower school director of curriculum. Unlike the other independent schools I visited, this school had many teachers and administrators who were struck by my diverse experiences. They were intrigued by the places I had visited—Spain, Cyprus, and Uzbekistan, to name a few. They wanted to know how it felt to leave home for a boarding school in India at the age of 11. Additionally, they valued my educational experiences in the fields of psychology and anthropology. At this particular independent school, it was clear that my life was important to them and I could be myself.

The opportunity to teach at an independent school was an opportunity to work with a population that I was familiar with. It also provided me with mentoring and training possibilities. Additionally, it was a setting in which I would be able to make a contribution, as a member of a minority ethnic group.

OUR DAY

Our morning in House 23 begins at 8:10 a.m. The children scuttle up the stairs from the lobby below. They hang up their coats and backpacks in their lockers located in the hallway and come into the room to begin their morning routines of signing in and working on the morning activity.

As their teacher, I wait at the front door or close to the door to greet them and help them if necessary. Our morning meeting, House as we call it, takes place at about 9:15 a.m. This is where we discuss the daily schedule and any special happenings. We may read our weekly poem together, or discuss a pattern in the calendar. Sometimes, we fulfill special projects such as the sharing of our Life Boxes, executed at the very beginning of the year.

Each child brings in a box with three to five items of particular importance to him or her. The items may be objects created or acquired, they may be photographs of special people or places, or they may be artifacts of milestones in the student's life. The children bring in their Life Boxes and share the contents with their classmates and teachers during the first 2 weeks of school. In this way we begin to build our classroom community as friends and learners. Through the sharing of these Life Boxes, individual interests and talents become evident. Similarities and differences in experiences also emerge, and the children connect on the common threads. The teachers in House 23 also create and talk about their own Life Boxes, as they too are part of the community.

One year, I was most struck by Anya's Life Box. Anya, of Indian descent, had spent the summer in India with her family. She returned to school full of stories of the places she had visited during her travels around the country. When she shared her Life Box, she began by noting the decorations on the outside. "These are pictures of Indian actors and actresses. I put them on the outside of the box, because this summer I saw lots of Hindi movies and had lots of fun." After our sharing session was over that day, Hannah went up to Anya and said, "Anya, I think it's really cool that you decorated your box with pictures of actors and actresses." Anya smiled in response, and so did I.

The rest of the day continues as the children and I move from one subject to another. Without any planning, opportune moments come up when we celebrate differences—not only based on ethnicity, but in terms of thinking, learning, and preferences as well.

At lunchtime one day, I heard Sam mockingly ask Keith, "Who's vegetarian?" I turned to face them and walked over closer to them. Keith was quiet, and I decided to intervene. I looked at Sam and most of the class, who by now had turned to look at the two boys, beckoned by Sam's loud and jarring tone of voice. "You know what, Sam, I'm vegetarian. I don't eat chicken, or beef—like hamburgers, or bacon, or even fish. But I do eat vegetables and beans and tofu. Does anyone know what tofu is?" The conversation between Sam and Keith turned into a whole-class celebration of different types of foods. Michael announced, "I drink only soy milk." Eliza stood up and said, "Sometimes I eat rice for breakfast." The children also asked me questions, "What did you eat for dinner every night, Ms. Awal?" and "What does tofu taste like?"

A few days later when the children had chicken nuggets for lunch, Sam came up to me to ask, "What will you eat, Ms. Awal?"

It perplexes me sometimes how, during my childhood, diversity of any kind was hidden. Maybe it just wasn't noticed, maybe it was something schools and educators believed was best ignored, or maybe the goal was to create classes of unified students who all fit into a mold. Many of the experiences I have had with my students have given me greater strength to share my own culture. Tara, whose mother is of Indian descent, came in one morning eager to teach her knowledge of the numbers in Bengali. "Do you know how to say the numbers in Hindi, Ms. Awal?" Her sincerity and the other children's intense curiosity got us talking about numbers in many, many different languages—Hebrew, Spanish, French, Japanese, Chinese, and, of course, Hindi, Bengali, and English. We ultimately made a list of the different numerical terms and used them during our weekly spelling tests. In my second-grade classroom at my elementary school, questions like these would never have been asked, and our natural curiosity about difference rarely saw the light.

MY COLLEAGUES

Unfortunately, the dialogue between my students and me is one that I do not yet have with my colleagues. When preparing for my first year as a head teacher, I was intrigued when I read in the curriculum guide that diversity was a concept that was focused on during social studies lessons in the spring semester. In subsequent grade-level meetings, when I questioned why diversity is focused on only at the end of the year, my colleagues did not seem to feel the same way. They support this set-up. Given my own experiences and commitment to diversity, I decided to make it an integral part of my curriculum. Furthermore, the examples above illustrate that diversity is not something that has been celebrated solely in the context of social studies. Some of my colleagues have come to me to discuss ideas on how to incorporate diversity into the curriculum in a more all-encompassing manner, yet many are resistant to change. Will faculty and administrators engage in possibly controversial and painful discourse in order to move forward in this vein?

WHERE ARE WE HEADED?

I'm encouraged by the openness that I have created in my classroom. I know that there are many independent school classrooms where diversity in human experience is embraced. In one room, children write poems to raise money for Kosovo; in another parents come in to help celebrate the Chinese and Indian (Diwali) new years. On the other hand, I am also painfully aware that there are many classrooms where the attitudes toward diversity, as modeled by the teachers, are much like those I experienced as a child.

There are times when I catch myself wishing for a more diverse group of children. A group of children from different countries, representing different religions and speaking different languages. I wonder if the scenario is any easier in a public school where the diversity in the population may be greater. But does a more diverse population mean that in public school classrooms diversity is celebrated more frequently or to a greater extent? Or are teachers in public schools aiming their efforts at helping their students assimilate into American society? I think the scenario is often the same. Some teachers, in both independent and public schools, have the inclination, the motivation, to include the lives of the children into the curriculum. From a faculty standpoint it seems that many more people of color (for lack of a better term) may be more easily granted a job at a public school and feel more accepted in a public school system. Yet it is the independent schools that often have greater resources to develop awareness among faculty, through workshops, presentations, school visits, and other means. But do these efforts alone increase the numbers of diverse faculty or make the curricula more all-encompassing in independent schools?

Will the 21st century see more widespread acceptance of difference in classrooms and schools across the country and the world? While I am encouraged by what I have seen so far, I realize that it will take a concerted effort on the part of all educators. Some may be motivated by their ethnic backgrounds, as I have been, while others will, ideally, find inspiration elsewhere.

Affirming Hispanic Co-workers in a School Community

Susana Epstein
Collegiate School, NY

During almost 20 years of teaching Spanish in New York City independent schools, one of my preoccupations as a Latina educator has been the validation of the Hispanic support staff employed at my schools. I have always been disturbed by the fact that kitchen and maintenance workers, receptionists, secretaries—employees without whom the institutions couldn't function properly—rarely are seen by students as relevant members of the school communities. As a matter of fact, I often have had the impression that these workers are all but invisible characters for many children. Do students know the names of the people who serve their meals, mail their reports, clean the building, or greet them everyday when they walk into school? Some do; the vast majority do not. Even worse, I wonder, do they care? Aware that the students' behavior toward these workers mirrors social attitudes that prevail in the broader spectrum of society, I have struggled to find ways to address and modify this injustice through my teaching.

Although not all school support staff is Hispanic at the Collegiate School, my current home, I felt that it was necessary for me to focus on my fellow Latinos, thus expanding my role as a Spanish teacher into the social studies field. My mission was twofold: educate students and affirm Hispanic co-workers.

Having embarked on several more or less successful attempts "to fix it" throughout my teaching career, after coming to Collegiate, an all-boys school, 4 years ago, I devised a strategy to make a difference. In my eleventh-grade Spanish course, I added a community component to the curriculum, which involved interviewing several Hispanic employees in our school. This teaching strategy was effective insofar as it encouraged the boys to re-examine their interaction with the school support staff and to know the staff as individuals, instead of as a collective of service providers. As an educated Hispanic, I felt it was my responsibility to be an agent of change within our school community.

While not giving a detailed account of each interview, I will describe what I consider the most meaningful stages of this project and share my findings. All quotations and translations are from my notes.

The 11 students in the class began by drafting questionnaires in Spanish, requesting general information such as, Where do you live? When did you come to the United States? as well as specific questions regarding the occupations of the people to be interviewed. We started by interviewing ourselves sitting in a circle, with each of us taking turns posing questions. This strategy allowed the students not only to practice Spanish and basic interviewing techniques but also to develop their critical thinking through discussions about the nature of public versus private information and the subsequent choices of topics they were required to make as interviewers. Even though we used our prepared questionnaires as frameworks in conducting the interviews, we also left room for spontaneous questions.

Next, we conducted "imaginary" interviews with popular figures, primarily from the sports and the arts worlds, before bringing in "real" guests. The boys at Collegiate tended to choose male figures, so we hosted baseball players, musicians, and politicians, often imitating familiar interviewing strategies from television. This was no doubt the most playful part of the project.

After that experience, I invited Violeta, my 22-year-old daughter, who is fully English–Spanish bilingual, to be interviewed. Violeta was the first interviewee from outside our classroom. I did not disclose our relationship. I did not give Violeta any special instructions. I told her only that I wanted her to come to my class to have students chat with a native speaker.

To my surprise, the students were initially shy and concerned with not looking silly by asking the wrong questions or using their Spanish incorrectly. I speculated that the reaction stemmed from their not being accustomed to encountering young women in a classroom. But when one student asked me, "Does she work here?" I realized that something else was happening. Instead of answering his question, I suggested he talk directly to our guest. The boy looked disoriented. How does one talk to the people that one does not normally acknowledge?

The students knew that our interviewee was not a teacher at Collegiate. Perhaps the other boys assumed that this dark-skinned young female worked in the kitchen or in one of the many offices in our school. When, after a while, somebody asked Violeta for her name, there was a dramatic change in the tone of the conversation. The students' body language became more relaxed, and most of them volunteered an array of questions. They were particularly impressed with the fact that my daughter had attended an Ivy League school and that she could speak both languages (especially English) without a foreign accent. In order to open up the conversation further, I asked Violeta to pose questions to the students. After this practice session, I felt we were ready to invite the first guest from our school community.

Samuel Pimentel, known affectionately to us as Sammy, the school driver and staff handyman, had been working at Collegiate for 29 years at the time he visited our class. Having learned what was effective and what was not by now, I structured the interview in much the same way as my daughter's visit, only this time I preferred to leave less room for the unexpected. I created a master questionnaire using the students' lists I previously had corrected, organizing the material sequentially. I also assigned specific questions to individual students to ensure that everybody had at least two turns to interact with our guest.

Sammy arrived at our classroom, initially looking very uncomfortable. Although I had described in detail what we would be doing, he obviously was not relaxed. In fact, at first he had been reluctant to come, not being fully convinced of the purpose of his visit. I welcomed him, and he sat down, looking around with uncertainty. The room was quiet. Sammy was not the only one feeling strange in the situation. As the students asked their prepared questions, Sammy gradually loosened up; he started to smile and speed up his talk. I even had to remind him that the boys were not fully fluent. Most of the time, he volunteered more information than the students' questions elicited. Halfway through, Sammy was cracking jokes, some containing culture-specific humor that I had to translate into English. There was a great deal of laughter. A couple of boys asked me if it was all right to ask Sammy additional questions—a request I had hoped for as an indicator of a successful session. With all the enthusiasm, I found it hard to wrap the meeting up.

As we thanked Sammy for his time, he asked if he could say a few words. He said that we did not need to thank him for anything, that indeed it was he who had to thank us for this opportunity: "You see, I look after these classrooms; I go in and out many times a day while classes are in progress, and I often wonder what do you kids do in these rooms. I know that you are doing something good because you are getting an education, but I do not know how you do it. I liked school when I was your age, but I never finished school. This is why I am here and you are there [pointing to the students]. I will never forget this occasion because for once I was part of what goes on in one of these rooms. I feel very honored." Uncertain of the appropriate response, most students simply left the room; a few shook Sammy's hand. One boy, visibly touched by Sammy's words, approached me and said, "This was our best Spanish class ever." Another one stopped me in the hallway to ask, "Can Sammy come again?"

When our class discussed Sammy's visit, the boys seemed moved by the encounter. One said that he was embarrassed to admit that he had been at Collegiate since first grade and had never spoken with Sammy until now. "Sammy must have driven me to hundreds of games and school trips," he said. "I must have seen him thousands of times around the school, and I didn't even know where he is from." (Most assumed that Sammy was from Puerto Rico and were surprised to learn he is from the Dominican Republic.)

They were also surprised when they asked Sammy where he lived and Sammy replied, "I live uptown, in the same building your teacher lives." He turned to me and continued, "You didn't tell them? We are neighbors." The entire group stared at me as if there were something wrong. Their reaction indicated to me that they thought Sammy and I could not be of the same kind. Yes, we are both Hispanic. We both work at Collegiate, but I am their teacher and Sammy is the bus driver and a handyman. Don't I make more money than him? How can we possibly live in the same building? Because I did not want to become too personal with my students, I preferred to leave them with some unanswered questions. I thought it was healthier for them to reflect on stereotypes.

It was not necessary to invite Sammy to class again. I began to catch students from my class chatting with Sammy. Our class project had forced them to pay attention to an individual who was very much part of their lives yet about whom they knew little or nothing. Once they discovered what a nice person Sammy is, they could not continue to ignore him.

Using a similar format, we next invited the school receptionist, German Llarch, who by then had been working at Collegiate for 7 years. Despite the fact that the nature of his job makes him more visible than Sammy, I suspected that there was much room for improvement in acknowledging German as an individual. German's politeness and great sense of responsibility are well known in the community. Morning through late evening he greets everybody with the friendliest expression; he receives the younger boys who arrive at school using a variety of bus services; he answers endless questions from parents, students, teachers, and delivery services; and he remains accountable for community safety by watching our main public entrance all day long. For me, one of German's most important roles is serving as a link between the administration and the Spanish-speaking maintenance staff. Primarily a Spanish speaker who has learned English in this country, German is the unofficial translator for many workers, especially for his father, Enrique, and younger brother, Pablo, who work in the building.

Unlike Sammy, German was relaxed from the beginning of the interview. Surprised that he knew all of their names, the students were even more surprised when they discovered that he knew the names of almost everybody in the school. Somebody asked German what he had done as a job before coming to Collegiate. "I was a croupier at a casino in Las Vegas," he explained. Impressed, one boy wondered if German could teach them some card tricks. "It wouldn't be appropriate in a school," said German with a smile.

In response to the boys' questions about the reasons that he, and so many other Dominicans, came to the United States, German spoke eloquently about the poverty on the island, the political and racial tension with Haiti, and many other topics that expanded the students' cultural understanding. For example, when German explained that he lived at home with his family as a single man in his thirties, the students were taken aback. I then explained that, although there have been changes, especially among Hispanics born in the United States, it is customary in Latin American countries to live at home until getting married. When I added that many Latin Americans don't even leave home to go to college, the boys couldn't repress their reactions. "That's stupid." "That's ridiculous." One student even asked whether we go to college at all. I assured them that we do, explaining that for us college is simply part of our schooling, simply one more school to go to. As we compared educational systems, I also explained the difficulty many Hispanic Americans may have getting used to living in an educational institution away from home.

Our interview grew into a lesson in social studies. I confirmed for myself that learning about cultural differences through an ongoing activity, rather than just reading or talking about them, is a powerful strategy for touching young minds. From then on, I knew my eleventh graders would not merely say a casual "Hi" to German on their way in or out of school. There was, in fact, a sense of complicity between German and these boys; they knew something about him that the rest of the student body most likely did not know. Priceless for me, they would always speak in Spanish to German, sometimes spending lengthy periods of time at his reception booth. By doing so, the students also were modeling behavior for the younger boys, who frequently tried to join in, to show off their own language skills or simply to talk with German.

I would have liked to interview other Hispanics at the school, but we ran out of time. Still, not only did we learn a lot from the interviews, but our discussions triggered other conversations about sexism, social class, race, cultural differences, and much more.

Sammy's and German's visits made a difference for my eleventh graders beyond Spanish class. The students, in turn, made a difference in the larger school community. Something else happened that I had not foreseen: Their visit affirmed me, in turn, as a Hispanic. My students learned information about me that they never would have heard otherwise; they participated in discussions about South Americans, Central Americans, people from the Caribbean, and Hispanic Americans (all of whom live under the label of Hispanics or Latinos) that changed the quality of our contact.

Now in college, several of these students continue to study Spanish and keep in touch with me. One, during the summer before going away to school, took German's position while German was on vacation. We talked a great deal about our interview with German, and I stopped by to ask him how he was doing in the job. He observed, "I admire German. I'd like to know how he manages to be so polite and helpful all day long. Half of the time I am ready to kill somebody; people ask me the stupidest things!"

I was happy with the results of this project. I wanted to render Hispanic co-workers visible to a community that does not seem to acknowledge them spontaneously, and my eleventh-grade class and I have succeeded. I wanted to grab the opportunity to become more visible myself, to be seen by my students in a new light—as a member of an ethnic group composed of multiple faces. What does it mean to be Hispanic or Latino, after all?

We spent several class periods looking into the subtleties of ethnic labeling. I took pleasure in the discussions that followed, feeling that it had been useful to all of us involved in this project—students, support staff, and myself—to be nudged out of our comfort zones. The exercise forced us to redefine the socially determined spaces within the school community. As we examined the ways in which the ethnic and social divisions simply reproduced what happens in our country on a larger scale, we began to explore the role of leaders who could narrow, open, or even erase such frontiers.

My students discovered that the term *Hispanic*, or any other ethnic label for that matter, refers to individuals, not only to faceless people that are "alike." In a changing society, where so many cultures coexist, I can only hope that this exercise has a long-term effect on their lives, particularly in regard to dispelling stereotypes.

I promised myself that I would continue to work on perfecting these interviews as educational tools to suit my ideal of teaching Spanish with a social agenda. Ultimately, my goal is not only to see my students become fluent in Spanish by the time they graduate from Collegiate. I also want them to know whose language they are learning and why they are learning it. I want them to respect the cultural wealth hidden in the terms *Hispanic* or *Latino*. Lastly, I prefer that the boys practice Spanish primarily in their own neighborhoods and school, where they can communicate with the people they are in contact with on a daily basis, rather than viewing foreign language study as merely a requirement to participate in study programs abroad.

CHAPTER 6

The Challenge of Diversifying Independent Schools

Pearl Rock Kane and Alfonso J. Orsini

The chapters in this book are intended to address the question of whether independent schools can be the excellent institutions they want to be, without having a truly diverse faculty. The authors have been decisive in their response. Increasing the number of teachers of color in schools is not just a good thing to do; it is essential to the education of students of all races and ethnicities and it is vital for the global community in which they will live. In this chapter we consider the imperative for diversity that is woven throughout the fabric of this book and address the question of what independent schools must do to attract and retain a diverse faculty, a task that is made increasingly difficult by a diminishing pool of applicants and a general teacher shortage. We conclude with specific suggestions for meeting that challenge by calling upon trustees, administrators, teachers, parents, and students to make their schools more receptive places for teachers of color.

The world our students are preparing to enter has changed dramatically in the past half century. It is no longer dominated by "WASP" elites with interlocking aristocratic families and it is no longer dominated by Whites.[1] Fully two-thirds of the world population are people of color who are exercising increasing influence on world politics, economics, and cultural life.[2] Since the mission statements of most independent schools include the goal of preparing young people to live, work, and lead successfully in a multiracial and multiethnic world, schools must provide a microcosm of that society.

Diversity provides the precondition for deepening student awareness of the feelings and perceptions of others and the possibility of achieving greater understanding. Increasing the numbers of students and teachers of color in independent schools is therefore essential for good education. Students of color and White students alike need positive role models that teachers of color provide. Engagement with culturally diverse teachers helps students develop a sense of tolerance toward differences and may assist in breaking down various kinds of negative stereotypes that students may have about people who are different from themselves.

As story author Dennis Bisgaard points out in "My Chance Encounter with Independent Schools," truly diverse schools are more tolerant places for all students. They are genuinely inclusive and accepting institutions in which all members of the community feel a sense of ownership, empowerment, and belonging. It is essential to emphasize that diversity pertains and belongs to all of us, no matter what our background and/or our racial and ethnic makeup happens to be.

In effective schools, all students are able to see themselves mirrored in the school's power structure and thereby are enabled to feel a sense of self-worth. As Shafia Zaloom observes in her story, "Dirty Knees":

> Olivia and Sarah deserve to know who they are and to feel safe and valued within the school community. They and their White classmates deserve an inclusive education that will empower them to embrace their own individuality and help them to live and work in a diverse society. . . . Schools can't only create space for people of color; they must empower them to move from the margins to the center.

But increasing the numbers of people of color in schools is simply not enough. The schools must provide an environment to which teachers of color are drawn and in which they are willing to stay. The research and the personal accounts presented in this book emphasize that increasing the numbers is only the first step in the long road toward making faculty of color receptive to a career in independent education. As our case studies and survey findings indicate, schools need to commit to transforming themselves into truly multicultural communities.

Schools that are likely to succeed in attracting and retaining faculty of color are embarking on school-wide change that involves scrutinizing every aspect of school life, including the explicit and the hidden curriculum. If we are serious about diversifying independent schools, then we must provide our students with a curriculum that allows for honest dialogue and critical thinking about our differences as well as our similarities. We need to examine and reflect on how classes of various levels are grouped and consider the patterns of participation in extracurricular activities.

Institutional change requires educating the entire community—trustees, administrators, teachers, staff, students, and parents—about race and ethnicity. The task is not simply to help teachers of color accommodate to the school. Nor is it to place teachers of color in situations where they are the cultural carriers—burdened with the task of teaching peers and students about diversity issues—often while, as young teachers, they too are in the process of working out their own identity. Our survey findings indicate that many teachers of color are asked to deal with a panoply of problems of students of color, while at the same time being held responsible for a full workload of other responsibilities. As Alexis Wright describes in "Excess Baggage":

I've had teachers ask me to speak to and mentor students of color who are in academic or social trouble, with the underlying assumption being that because the student and I might have the same skin color, then surely I can make a connection that others have not been able to make. Never mind that the student may have a totally different background from mine, or may be in a different division of the school, or that I have a full schedule and my own advisees to worry about. Our race might be the only common denominator, but it is assumed that all problems will be solved.

Whole-school change involves recognition that diversity is everyone's job. The over 90% of White teachers in independent schools must be educated to take responsibility for challenging racism in their classrooms and in their schools. Professor James Banks points out: "It is essential for us to explore the changes and growth that must take place in White educators in order for them to help create caring and humane schools."[3] White educators need to confront their White privilege and racism so that they become partners and leaders in creating multicultural schools.[4] As Erik Resurreccion points out in his story, "How Did I End Up Here," this transformation requires time and effort.

Part of the problem is that independent schools tend to believe in the "silver bullet theory." Faculty and administrators in schools claim they had a workshop a couple of years ago and devoted a series of faculty meetings to issues of diversity. A "been there done that" attitude pervades some independent schools that have been exposed to the issues of diversity without substantial follow-up and action steps. Making significant progress in diversifying schools requires a great deal of courage and commitment to drastically change the culture of the school, and hard work to sustain it.

Change also requires attention to political dynamics, identifying the power centers of the school. If the board, the administration, or the parent body is controlling the school on matters of diversity, then that group must be fully in agreement on where the school is headed. Schools need to decide just how diverse they are willing to become.

Pia Awal asks in "The Journey of an Indian American Student and Teacher":

> Will the 21st century see widespread acceptance of difference in classrooms and schools across the country and the world? While I am encouraged by what I have seen so far, I realize that it will take a concerted effort on the part of all educators. Some may be motivated by their ethnic backgrounds, as I have been, while others will, ideally, find inspiration elsewhere.

The argument of this book is that until independent schools succeed in creating positive cultures sensitive to and accepting of different races and ethnicities, they will fall short of providing an optimal education for all students. The chapters in this book contain suggestions for ways to achieve that goal. In the interim, independent schools are fortunate to have attracted a cadre of teachers of color who are trail blazers in helping to bring about the transformation process. As author Mariah Childs observes:

> Teaching at an independent school is a personal challenge. Those of us who choose this path leave the "many" students of color in public school to help the "few" students of color who attend independent schools. In doing so, we give the gift of ourselves to students and faculty who may not otherwise have the opportunity for dialogue or fellowship with talented professionals of color. Through our voices and our presence on independent school campuses, faculty of color have the opportunity to educate, stimulate, and help eradicate misconceptions, stereotypes and racist notions about non-Europeans.

As educators, we are in positions to enlighten the minds of students, many of whom will eventually hold politically and economically powerful positions, and whose decisions may impact the lives of people of color throughout the world.

As teachers of color we must not take lightly this mantle that has been placed upon us. Though we may be few in number, we can be mighty in influence. As faculty and staff of color, we bring reality into the lives of students, staff and faculty who might otherwise not need to step outside of their comfort zone to gain greater awareness and understanding of people who do not look like them or share similar cultural backgrounds. Through our very presence we teach. Through our actions we help to open doors of accessibility, trust and eventually acceptance. We must not give up! The struggle continues but the battle is not over.

FINDING TEACHING CANDIDATES OF COLOR

To meet the philosophical imperative of diversifying independent school faculties, a school must consider what practical steps it can take. Thus we end this chapter by offering a review of the most salient pieces of advice that have been gathered through our various studies. But we caution that there is no quick fix to ensure diversity, just a great deal of work, but work that will benefit all members of a school community.

Revive Face-to-Face Campus Recruitment

The first step in the process of diversifying a faculty is to know how and where to seek teaching candidates of color. Before independent school teacher agencies existed, representatives from independent schools went to colleges to recruit firsthand. While agencies may succeed in recruiting able candidates generally, the recruitment of teachers of color will require a more concerted and more personal effort. The agencies and recruitment organizations consulted in this study clearly expressed their sense of frustration both with finding candidates of color and with convincing independent schools to recognize the candidates' talents and credentials. Various explorations in this project clearly have suggested that face-to-face recruitment by independent school administrators and teachers may be the most effective means of finding candidates of color. While people who work in independent schools may live and work under the assumption that the general public knows all about them, this belief has proven to be inaccurate. In fact, since only a minuscule portion of American children attend independent schools, very few people are familiar with them. For many Americans, perhaps more so for Americans of color, if they know about independent schools at all, they may know them merely as brick structures with nice lawns and gates that one passes on the road. They may appear simply as clubbish places for wealthy kids.

Independent school educators may need to take their message on the road and out into the community. They might follow the lead of business organizations and successful endeavors such as Teach for America by having teachers, particularly young teachers of color, involved in campus recruitment of teachers of color. Young recruits will benefit from learning firsthand about the mission and culture of the school, its aims and values, its curriculum, and the extent to which it values and welcomes diversity. If young people of color feel some trepidation at entering what they view as an elite and exclusive world, even the best-intentioned agency recruiter will not reverse that view. Candidates of color need to feel that they will be welcomed and valued and supported, rather than to suspect that they are intruders into an alien world.

Network with Parents

This study also has suggested that networking with parents, particularly parents of color, may be a vital step in finding candidates of color, especially since so many current teachers of color have found their jobs through a previous association with the school. In their affiliations with churches and other community and cultural groups, parents of color can connect the school with a number of people it otherwise might never know. Significantly, parents and teachers are invited to become partners in the school-wide work of fostering diversity, and that work becomes part of the fabric of the school rather than a mysterious process that a few administrators may or may not be actively pursuing in private.

Develop Community Collaborations

Our studies also suggest that independent schools can attract more candidates of color by reaching out and opening their doors to the wider community. Schools can create collaboratives with local public schools and other organizations to break down the veil of exclusion and mystery that often surrounds independent schools. One of the most striking examples in this study is the creation of summer programs that bring members of the surrounding community into the school, especially families and teachers from public schools. Cultural and multicultural events such as arts performances, speakers, and open forum discussions also can reverse an image of the school as a "private" place and at the same time can send the clear message that the school values diversity. Our survey of teachers of color at independent schools suggested that these teachers are more likely to stay at a school that is involved with a public school.

Recruit Alumni/ae of Color

Both our surveys and the personal vignettes submitted suggest that many teachers of color took their first job at their alma mater. The attraction of teachers of color to their former schools or to other independent schools is enhanced when alums recall that at independent schools teachers are valued, respected, and honored in everyday life, in assemblies, through annual awards, and through students', parents', and administrators' constant reminders of the valuable work that teachers do. If we ever hope to attract students of color back to their independent schools to teach, they will need to view independent schools as places where diversity is valued in everyday life.

Cast a Wider Net in Advertising

Finally, by moving beyond merely placing openings with agencies and hoping for the best, schools can place ads in local newspapers focused on African American, Asian, and Latino audiences. Teachers also can be encouraged to reach out to graduate school classmates, friends, and acquaintances from conferences to help generate more candidates of color. The more people involved collaboratively in the work of diversity, the better. Even if the collective efforts do not immediately succeed, at least everyone will know that a genuine effort is being made. And instead of paying agencies, schools could be offering finder's fees to teachers, parents, and students who help in the hiring of teachers.

THE HIRING PROCESS

Look beyond Superficial Qualifications

This study has clearly suggested that those responsible for hiring at independent schools (heads, academic deans, department chairs) should not set qualifications artificially high, such as an Ivy League degree and middle-class background or a diploma from an independent school, as often seems to be the case with the practice for hiring current independent school teachers of color. While little research has been done on the educational backgrounds of independent and public school teachers, the sample in Kane's 1986 study suggested that 60% of independent school teachers had attended colleges classified as "very competitive" or "most competitive." However, these statistics do not indicate that one has to be a graduate of an Ivy League school in order to successfully teach in an independent school, even if parents do scrutinize such issues in their shopping for schools. A quality teaching staff is crucial to the success of independent schools, but quality is not always easily equated with credentials.

Make Interviews an Inviting Two-way Process

The interview process needn't be merely a narrowly defined inspection of candidates. Candidates need to feel they are entering a welcome, humane environment. If the interview process is conducted as an inspection of whether candidates fit a predetermined prototype of "the independent school teacher," then they will sense that they are not being valued for their unique, diverse talents. They will sense that they are being measured and tested. The implicit question in such narrowly conducted interviews is not, "What can you bring and add to what already exists here?" but rather, "How will you fit in with what already exists here?" That can be the first and fundamental denial of diversity that the candidate experiences. It can be the one that irrevocably and understandably turns the candidate away from the school. If schools can feel secure only if they hire middle-class candidates of color with all the "right" credentials to satisfy nervous parents, then the groundwork for true diversity has not been successfully laid.

Involve Teachers, Students, and Parents in the Interview Process

The interview process should include meeting other teachers, especially teachers of color, to understand what daily life is like at the school. Interviews by administrators and department chairs may mask the very different daily experience of teachers, especially teachers of color. Candidates, in the view of interviewed teachers of color currently working in independent schools, should meet students and parents, especially parents and students of color, during the interview process. If the school cannot invite teachers, parents, and students to talk freely with candidates about the culture and daily life of the school, then perhaps the fundamental work of honoring diversity at the school has not yet been done.

RETAINING TEACHERS OF COLOR

Ensure that Leaders Openly and Clearly Commit to Diversity

The board and head must make evident to the school and the larger communities that they value and are actively engaged in building diversity. When parents express suspicions of or complaints about teachers of color, department chairs and administrators must be skillful at sensing discrimination and be ready to defend good teachers who are being questioned because of race rather than ability. Indeed, all members of the school community must be ready to stand up to inappropriate comments and behavior from anyone in the community.

Involve the Diversity Coordinator in Decision Making

A diversity coordinator, if such a person is designated, should be part of the head of school's "cabinet" and have access to and influence in decision making. And the diversity coordinator should not become the only person in the school working at fostering diversity and the embracing of difference. That should be everyone's work, with the diversity coordinator as the "point person" in conjunction with the admissions staff, the people who hire, the people who devise curriculum, the academic staff, and even the board of trustees.

Set Measurable Institutional Goals and Communicate on Progress

The head of school and board of trustees, after taking the time to educate themselves about diversity, should confront the issue of how diverse they are willing to allow the school to be. They then need to set measurable institutional goals that they can communicate to and discuss with the entire school community. The board can begin by looking at the composition of its own membership. The head of school can look at the composition of the administrative team. Clear communication of the school's agenda and goals is crucial because more often than not, a void of information and communication becomes filled with suspicion and cynicism. To maintain the integrity of the school's commitment, the school should make available, at least to its faculty, statistics on openings, interviews conducted, and positions filled. The school community needs to know the efforts being made to diversify the faculty. And the school must constantly benchmark and self-reflect on its progress toward its goals. The school's commitment to diversity and intercultural understanding should be expressed clearly in all of its literature, at open house presentations, and in every facet of daily life. Any outsider or visitor should know the school's stance on diversity. As noted below, commitment is also evident in the way a school allocates resources.

Provide Comprehensive Orientation

All teachers, and perhaps particularly teachers of color and others who are new to independent schools, benefit from having a thorough orientation to the school's mission and culture and to the idiosyncrasies of its everyday life. This orientation needs to be followed up with structured, comprehensive mentoring, even of experienced teachers new to the independent school world. Comprehensive mentoring programs, such as the one established at Lawrenceville School, provide mentors with training and guidelines for their work, define the relationship between mentor and new teacher, state the connection of mentoring to the evaluation process, and provide adequate time and compensation to mentors.

Don't Overburden Teachers of Color

If independent schools hope to retain teachers of color, they need to ensure that dealing with diversity is part of every teacher's responsibilities. The one or two teachers of color on staff, as is often the case currently, cannot be called upon to handle every racial issue, to deal with the problems of every student of color, to be the main line of communication with parents of color, or to organize every multicultural assembly and club. Young teachers of color are already faced with the struggle of trying to hone their skills in a new profession.

Scrutinize Curriculum for Inclusiveness

Effective schools treat the curriculum as a live document, one that is continually being reviewed in terms of meeting the school's objectives. Part of the school's ongoing assessment should be a consideration of the extent to which the curriculum is inclusive and the extent to which it fosters intercultural understanding. A useful exercise carried out by at least one school visited was the mapping of the entire curriculum to study the degree to which it is genuinely multicultural.

Make Exposure to and Awareness of Diversity a Way of Life

Through activities, trips, and community, students need to be exposed to people different from themselves, especially the people of color who statistically make up such a large portion of support staff at NAIS schools, as Susana

Epstein's story suggests. But no amount of exposure to diverse people outside the community can counterbalance a glaring lack of diversity among the people in the community who most seriously influence and affect students: their teachers.

Make an Ongoing Commitment to Anti-bias and Diversity Training

All teachers, administrators, students, and parents need to be exposed to anti-bias training and to issues of diversity on an ongoing basis, not just through a one-time presentation. They also need to be made aware of what it means to be a student or teacher of color in a largely White environment. People's voices from every part of the community need to be heard, for nothing speaks more strongly than firsthand sharing of experiences and perspectives from people both within and outside the community. As one interviewee stated, "Recognize difference; don't pamper it." Until the school is a truly multicultural environment that acknowledges and honors diversity, one cannot expect teachers of color to enter independent schools or to stay in them if they discover a grim reality.

Ensure Excellent Salary and Benefits

The first step in hiring and retaining any teachers, but perhaps more so capable people of color who are now more than ever being sought by other professions eager to diversify, is to ensure excellent salary and benefits. One benefit that appears to matter most is tuition scholarships for children of teachers. More than ever, as numbers of teachers dwindle and many in the teaching force approach retirement, independent schools are competing with public schools and other industries to attract capable people.

Devote Resources to Financial Aid for Students of Color

Boards of trustees and heads of school also must give priority to raising money for financial aid to students of color, another major step in the effort to diversify in that it builds the critical mass of students of color and says to candidates that the school values diversity. Candidates of color feel that they have an important role to play in a school with a diverse student body and that there is at least a community of students and parents with whom they can feel a more immediate affinity. The strongest correlations of factors in our study of NAIS statistics were those between percentage of students of color and percentage of faculty of color and between percentage of students of color and percentage of financial aid given to students of color.

Fund professional development

Independent schools need to offer support for graduate study that permits career building and enhancement, as well as support for culturally and educationally relevant professional development. Schools should consider offering a bonus to teachers who spare the school's professional development budget by finding outside funding for professional development through scholarships or grants such as those provided by the National Endowment for the Humanities or the National Science Foundation. Independent schools need to show that they make diversity a priority by devoting resources to it, even scarce resources. Interestingly, some of the most well-endowed NAIS schools in our study were among the least diverse, while schools with small endowments were among the most diverse.

Diversifying independent school faculties will take a great deal of thought and planning, and it also will require commitment and action. As this study has suggested, the key seems to be getting beyond having only one or two faculty members of color (or none as in a tragically large number of schools) to reach a critical mass into which more students and faculty of color can enter with assurance and hope. Perhaps the greatest care must be taken and the most serious work done by every member of the community in the early phases, before diversity can begin to beget diversity.

By their very nature, independent schools historically have cultivated their exclusivity through their pursuit of excellence. This factor has tended to make potential clients want them more, clients who traditionally have been White people with resources. The question in the decades ahead will be whether independent schools can change with a demographically changing America, whether they can alter their conception of excellence and their complexion to match a nation and a world that are poised to become one people with many faces and many cultures. If they do not change as such, they soon may find that their missions are antiquated and they no longer are meeting their promise of preparing young people to excel in and contribute to the world at large. In this regard, a diverse independent school is the best school for everyone connected with it, and even for the many millions of people who will never attend or even visit an independent school but who certainly will work and live beside those who have attended independent schools.

Notes

Introduction

1. Many of these schools have religious roots and traditions, but function primarily as nonsectarian institutions, particularly with respect to admissions and hiring policies.

2. National Association of Independent Schools (2000), Table 3, p. 10.

3. Tatum, B. D. (1997); McIntosh, P. (1988).

Chapter 1

1. National Association of Independent Schools (1999), Table 13.

2. Pflaum, S., & Abramson, T. (1990), p. 19.

3. National Center for Education Statistics (1999), Table 99.

4. Findings are from a 1990 study by the National Opinion Research Center at the University of Chicago as reported in Schevtchuk-Armstrong, L. (1991).

5. Grant, C. A. (1990), p. 27.

6. Stevens, L. B. (1996).

7. Parks-Daloz, L. (1996).

8. King, S. (1991); Grant (1990).

9. Cole, B. P. (1986); Spellman, S. O. (1988), pp. 58-63.

10. King (1991), p. 79, citing a 1986 Carnegie Forum assessment.

11. Middleton, E. J., Mason, E. J., Stillwell, W. E., & Parker, C. (1988), pp. 14-18.

12. National Association of Independent Schools (2000), p. 23.

13. Aitken, H. P., et al. (1994).

14. Banks, J. A., & Banks, C. A. (1989); Darling-Hammond, L., Dilworth, M. E., & Bullmaster, M. L. (1996).

15. Bass de Martinez, B. (1988), p. 13.

16. Dilworth, M. E. (1988), p. ix.

17. Dilworth, M. E. (1988), p. 6.

18. Delpit, L. (1986).

19. Murell, P. C., Jr. (1994), p. 567.

20. Delpit, L. (1988).

21. Ladson-Billings, G. (1994).

22. Shade, B. J., & New, C. A. (1989).

23. Comprehensive reviews of research have been provided by King, S. (1993), pp. 115-149; Irvine, J. J. (1988), pp. 503-513; Darling-Hammond et al. (1996).

151

24. Beady, C. H., & Hansell, S. (1987), pp. 191–206.

25. Kash, M. M., & Borich, G. D. (1978).

26. Davidson, H. H., & Lang, G. (1960), pp. 107–118; Rosenthal, R., & Jacobsen, L. F. (1968), pp. 19–22.

27. Feldman, R. S., & Donohoe, L. F. (1978), pp. 979–987.

28. Simpson, A. W., & Erickson, M. T. (1983), pp. 183–198.

29. Simpson & Erickson (1983), p. 183.

30. Washington, V. (1980), p. 200.

31. Holliday, B. G. (1985), p. 79.

32. Anderson, J. A. (1988).

33. Interviews were held at Teachers College, Columbia University, during the 1997–1998 academic year. The duration of the interviews was approximately one and a half hours. Those interviewed for this project and the organizations they were affiliated with at the time included: Dennis Bisgaard, Director, The Collegiate Teaching Institute; Randolph Carter, Director of Diversity and Multicultural Services, The National Association of Independent Schools; Rachel Conescu, Program Officer, The Dewitt Wallace Readers Digest Fund; Kevin Franklin, President, The Multicultural Alliance; Susan Hinkle, Director, Diversity Resources; John Hoffman, President, The Independent Teaching Project; Annette Lieberson, Executive Director, The Interschool Program; and, Verne Oliver, The Manhattan Institute.

34. Interviewers included Professor Pearl Rock Kane and graduate students Jan Scott, Michelle Smith, Lynn Sorensen, and Danielle Wilcox.

35. Presley, C. (1991), p. 28.

36. Edelman, J. (1993), p. 45.

Chapter 2

1. U.S. Census Bureau (2002), Table 15.

2. U.S. Census Bureau (2002), Table 15.

3. U.S. Census Bureau (2002), Table 24.

4. Betty, S. (1990), p. 52.

5. Haberman, M. (1998), p. 38.

6. Spellman, S. O. (1988).

7. National Center for Education Statistics (1995).

8. National Center for Education Statistics (1999), p. 126.

9. Bradley, A. (1991), pp. 19–20.

10. U.S. Census Bureau (1996), Table 49.

11. U.S. Census Bureau (1999), Table B5.

12. U.S. Census Bureau (1999), Table B5.

13. U.S. Census Bureau (1996), Table 53.

14. U.S. Census Bureau (1996), Table 50.

15. Darling-Hammond et al. (1996); Murnane, R. J., Singer, J. D., Willet, J. B., Kemple, J. J., & Olsen, R. J. (1991).

16. Darling-Hammond et al. (1996), p. 23.

17. Darling-Hammond et al. (1996), p. 47.

18. All figures are based on Table 1, pp. 54-55 in Carter, D. J., & Wilson, R. (1995).

19. National Center for Education Statistics (1999), Table 209.

20. American Association of Colleges for Teacher Education (1994), Table 3, p. 8.

21. American Association of Colleges for Teacher Education (1994), Table II, p. 14.

22. National Center for Education Statistics (1995), Table 261, p. 288.

23. National Center for Education Statistics (1999), Table 207.

24. Darling-Hammond et al. (1996), p. 44.

25. Bobbitt, S., et al. (1995), Table 66, p. 77.

26. National Center for Education Statistics (1998) Table 7.6, p. 146.

27. National Center for Education Statistics (1995), Table 72, p. 81.

28. National Center for Education Statistics (2000), Table 70.

29. National Center for Education Statistics (1995), Table 71, p. 81.

30. National Center for Education Statistics (1995), Tables 39-40, pp. 333-334.

31. National Center for Education Statistics (1999), Table 270.

32. Kane, P. R. (1990), p. 805.

33. Haberman, M. (1989), p. 773.

34. King (1993), p. 136; see also Graham, P. A. (1987), pp. 598-605.

35. Haberman (1989), p. 772.

36. Gordon, J. A. (1994), p. 348.

37. Darling-Hammond et al. (1996), p. 33.

38. Gifford, B. R. (1986), pp. 251-271; Irvine (1988); Cooper, C. C. (1986), pp. 46-55; Smith, G. P. (1987); Smith, G. P. (1988), pp. 45-53.

39. Cole (1986); Irvine (1988).

40. Murnane, R. J., & Philips, B. R. (1991), pp. 83-100; Cole (1986).

41. Johnson, S. T., & Prom-Jackson, S. (1986), p. 279.

42. Gifford (1986), pp. 270-271; see also Tanner, D. E. (1986), pp. 13-17.; Cooper (1986); Spellman (1988); Sherman, T. M., Giles, M., & Williams-Green, J. (1994), pp. 164-179.

43. Phone interview with Carter, D. J., American Council on Education, Office of Minorities in Higher Education, June 24, 1996.

44. Dilworth (1988).

45. Gordon (1994), p. 350.

46. Perkins, L. M. (1989).

47. King (1991), pp. 138-139.

48. King (1993), pp. 115-149.

49. King (1991), p. 31.

50. Chinn, P. C., & Wong, G. Y. (1992), p. 124.

51. American Association of Colleges for Teacher Education, (1994); Garibaldi, A. M. (1989); Witty, E. P. (1989) Graham (1987).

52. Darling-Hammond et al. (1996).

53. Worner, R. B. (1991); and Grier, T. B. (1993), pp. 44-46.

54. Gonzalez, J. M. (1996).

55. Richardson, J. (1995), p. 24.
56. Smith, A. L. (1990), pp. 43–45.
57. National Education Association (1996), p. 52.
58. Powell, A. (1996), p. 85.
59. Powell (1996), pp. 89–90.
60. Powell (1996), p. 86.
61. Kraushaar, O. F. (1972), p. 240.
62. Mallery, D. (1963), pp. 14–15.
63. Powell (1996), p. 97.
64. Powell (1996), p. 98.
65. Wilson, Z. V. (1983), p. x.
66. Wilson (1983), p. xi.
67. Wilson (1983), p. 47.
68. National Association of Independent Schools (2002).
69. Dandridge, W. L. (1978), p. 8.
70. National Association of Independent Schools (1996).
71. National Association of Independent Schools (1999).

Chapter 3

1. The authors wish to thank Randolph Carter, Director of Diversity and Multicultural Services at NAIS, for his assistance in conducting and interpreting the teacher of color survey.

2. National Association of Independent Schools (1999), Table 13.

3. U.S. Census Bureau (1999), Table NPD1A.

4. The sample was obtained by using the 1997 NAIS mailing list of 430 diversity coordinators and contact people. We asked the coordinators and contacts to distribute the surveys to teachers of color in their schools. We received 691 surveys representing 21% of the total teachers of color in independent schools, according to NAIS statistics.

5. Rosabeth Moss Kanter in *Men and Women of the Corporation* (1977), discusses the impact that the relative size of a subgroup has on the cultural understanding of the entire group. In short, "token minorities" are more likely to be misunderstood and stereotyped, and their individual characteristics taken as representative of characteristics of their cultural group at large. The larger a subgroup becomes within a community, the less likely the majority population is to mistake individual differences for cultural traits.

6. At the 16 schools in Hawaii and the U.S. Territories, 71% of all students and 26% of all teachers are people of color. Of course, this meant removing some 9,593 students of color and 306 teachers of color from the NAIS numbers. But if Hawaii comprises 70% people of color, among whom 59% are Asian/Pacific Islander, then perhaps we should be looking at statistics on people of non-color.

7. Walsh, M. (1991), pp. 8–9.

8. Correlations were: starting salary .22 (α <.025); median salary .22 (α <.025); % financial aid to students of color .35 (α <.005), and % students of color .44 (α <.005).

9. U.S. Census Bureau (1990). To find all the zip codes in a 20-mile radius of each school, we used the Map Info Program.

10. Correlations were: total population .29 (α <.005); % urban population .28 (α <.005); % people of color in population .39 (α <.005).

11. Kane (1990).

Chapter 4

1. One team was able to interview only one of the two teachers at one of its schools. The final tally of interviews included the head of each of the 11 schools, the director of diversity (or similar person), and two teachers of color, with the solitary exception just noted, for a total of 43 interviews.

2. Interschool is a consortium of independent day schools in New York City that sponsors the Interschool Teaching Fellows Program. Initiated in 1984, the program offers recent college graduates an opportunity to gain a supervised teaching internship experience to prepare them for a career in teaching.

Chapter 5

1. Senge, P. M. (1990).

Chapter 6

1. Brooks, D. (2000).

2. Kennedy, P. A. (1993), points out that between now and 2030, 95% of the world's population growth will occur in developing nations.

3. Banks, J. A. (1999).

4. Tatum, B. D. (1997); McIntosh, P. (1988).

References

Aitken, H. P., et al. (1994). *Access and affordability: Strategic financial perspective for independent schools*. Washington, DC: National Association of Independent Schools.

American Association of Colleges for Teacher Education (1994). *Teacher education pipeline III: Schools, colleges, and departments of education, enrollments by race, ethnicity, and gender*. Washington, DC: Author.

Anderson, J. A. (1988). Cognitive styles and multicultural populations. *Journal of Teacher Education, 39*(1), 2-9.

Banks, J. A. (1999). Series foreword. In G. R. Howard, *We can't teach what we don't know: White teachers in multiracial schools* (pp. ix-xi). New York: Teacher College Press.

Banks, J. A., & Banks, C. A. (Eds.). (1989). *Multicultural education: Issues and perspectives*. Boston: Allyn & Bacon.

Bass de Martinez, B. (1988). Political and reform agendas' impact on the supply of Black teachers. *Journal of Teacher Education, 39*(1), 10-13.

Beady, C. H., & Hansell, S. (1987). Teacher race and expectation for student achievement. *American Educational Research Journal, 18*, 191-206.

Betty, S. (1990). *New strategies for producing minority teachers: Technical report*. Denver, CO: Education Commission of the States.

Bobbitt, S., et al. (1995). *Schools and staffing in the United States: Selected data for public and private schools, 1993-94* (NCES Document No. 95-191). Washington, DC: U.S. Department of Education.

Bradley, A. (1991, May 15). Newly diverse suburbs facing city style woes. *Education Week*, pp. 19-20.

Brooks, D. (2000). *Bobos in paradise: The new upper class and how they got there*. New York: Simon & Schuster.

Carter, D. J., American Council on Education, Office of Minorities in Higher Education. Phone interview, June 24, 1996.

Carter, D. J., & Wilson, R. (1995). *Minorities in higher education: Fourteenth annual status report*. Washington, DC: American Council on Education.

Chinn, P. C., & Wong, G. Y. (1992). Recruiting and retaining Asian/Pacific American teachers. In M. E. Dilworth (Ed.), *Diversity in teacher education: New expectations* (pp. 112-133). San Francisco: American Association of Colleges for Teacher Education/Jossey-Bass.

Cole, B. P. (1986). The Black educator: An endangered species. *Journal of Negro Education, 55,* 326-334.

Cooper, C. C. (1986). Strategies to assure certification and retention of Black teachers. *Journal of Negro Education, 55*(1), 46-55.

Dandridge, W. L. (1978). Recruiting minority teachers of independent schools. *Independent School, 38*(2), 8-11.

Darling-Hammond, L., Dilworth, M. E., & Bullmaster, M. L. (1996). Background paper for the invitational conference, Recruiting, Preparing, and Retaining Persons of Color in the Teaching Profession, January 22-24, 1996. Manuscript prepared in cooperation with the Office of Educational Research and Improvement, U.S. Department of Education.

Davidson, H. H., & Lang, G. (1960). Children's perceptions of their teacher's feelings of them related to self-perception, school achievement, and behavior. *Journal of Experimental Education, 29,* 107-118.

Delpit, L. (1986). Skills and other dilemmas of a progressive Black educator. *Harvard Educational Review, 56*(4), 379-385.

Delpit, L. (1988). The silenced dialogue: Power and pedagogy in educating other people's children. *Harvard Educational Review, 58*(3), 280-298.

Dilworth, M. E. (1988). Black teachers: A vanishing tradition. *The Urban League Review, 2*(12), 54-58.

Edelman, J. (1993, Spring). Multicultural responsibility. *Independent School, 52,* 43-45.

Feldman, R. S., & Donohoe, L. F. (1978). Nonverbal communication of affect in interracial dyads. *Journal of Educational Psychology, 70*(6), 979-987.

Garibaldi, A. M. (Ed.). (1989). *Teacher recruitment and retention: With a special focus on minority teachers.* Washington, DC: National Education Association.

Gifford, B. R. (1986). Excellence and equity in teacher competency testing: A policy perspective. *Journal of Negro Education, 55*(3), 251-271.

Gonzalez, J. M. (1996). *Recruiting and retaining minority leaders: Student views of pre-service programs.* Unpublished manuscript.

Gordon, J. A. (1994). Why students of color are not entering teaching: Reflections from minority teachers. *Journal of Teacher Education, 45*(5), 346-353.

Graham, P. A. (1987). Black teachers: A drastically scarce resource. *Phi Delta Kappan, 68*(8), 598-605.

Grant, C. A. (1990). Desegregation, racial attitudes, and intergroup contact: A discussion of change. *Phi Delta Kappan, 71*(1), 27.

Grier, T. B. (1993, November). Diversity becomes us. *American School Board Journal, 180,* 44-46.

Haberman, M. (1989, June). More minority teachers. *Phi Delta Kappan, 70,* 771-776.

Haberman, M. (1998, July). Proposals for recruiting minority teachers: Promising practices and attractive detours. *Journal of Teacher Education, 39*(4), 38-44.

Holliday, B. G. (1985). Differential effects of children's self-perceptions and teachers' perceptions on Black children's academic achievement. *Journal of Negro Education, 54,* 71-81.

Irvine, J. J. (1988). An analysis of the problem of disappearing Black educators. *Elementary School Journal, 88*, 503-513.

Johnson, S. T., & Prom-Jackson, S. (1986). The memorable teacher: Implications for teacher selection. *Journal of Negro Education, 55*, 272-283.

Kane, P. R. (1990, June). Just ask liberal arts graduates to teach. *Phi Delta Kappan, 71*, 805-807.

Kanter, R. M. (1977). *Men and women of the Corporation.* New York: Basic Books.

Kash, M. M., & Borich, G. D. (1978). *Teacher behavior and pupil self concept.* Reading, MA: Addison-Wesley.

Kennedy, P. A. (1993). *Preparing for the twenty-first century.* New York: Vintage Press.

King, S. (1991). *Exploring the early career experiences of African American teachers.* Unpublished doctoral dissertation, Teachers College, Columbia University.

King, S. (1993). The limited presence of African American teachers. *Review of Educational Research, 63*(2), 115-149.

Kraushaar, O. F. (1972). *American non-public schools: Patterns of diversity.* Baltimore: Johns Hopkins University Press.

Ladson-Billings, G. (1994). *The dreamkeepers: Successful teachers of African American children.* San Francisco: Jossey-Bass.

Mallery, D. (1963). *Negro students in independent schools.* Boston: National Association of Independent Schools.

McIntosh, P. (1988). *White privilege: Unpacking the invisible knapsack.* Wellesley: Author.

Middleton, E. J., Mason, E. J., Stillwell, W. E., & Parker, C. (1988). A model for recruitment and retention of minority students in teacher preparation programs. *Journal of Teacher Education, 39*(1), 14-18.

Murell, P. C., Jr. (1994). In search of responsive teaching for African American males: An investigation of students' experiences of middle school mathematics curriculum. *Journal of Negro Education, 63*(4), 556-569.

Murnane, R. J., & Philips, B. R. (1991). What do effective teachers of inner city children have in common? *Social Science Research, 10*, 83-100.

Murnane, R. J., Singer, J. D., Willet, J. B., Kemple, J. J., & Olsen, R. J. (1991). *Who will teach?* Cambridge, MA: Harvard University Press.

National Association of Independent Schools. (1996). *The NAIS statistics.* Washington, DC: Author.

National Association of Independent Schools. (1999). *The NAIS statistics.* Washington, DC: Author.

National Association of Independent Schools. (2000). *The NAIS statistics.* Washington, DC: Author.

National Association of Independent Schools. (2002). *The NAIS statistics.* Washington, DC: Author.

National Center for Education Statistics. (1995). *The condition of education.* Washington, DC: U.S. Department of Education, Office of Educational Research and Improvement.

National Center for Education Statistics. (1995). *Digest of education statistics*. Washington, DC. U.S. Department of Education.

National Center for Education Statistics. (1998). *Schools and staffing survey 1993–1994*. Washington DC: U.S. Department of Education.

National Center for Education Statistics. (1999). *The condition of education*. Washington, DC: U.S. Department of Education.

National Center for Education Statistics. (1999). *Digest of education statistics*. Washington, DC: U.S. Department of Education.

National Center for Education Statistics. (2000). *The condition of education 2000* (NCES Document No. 2000-602). Washington, DC: U.S. Department of Education.

National Center for Education Statistics. (2000). *Digest of education statistics*. Washington DC: U.S. Department of Education.

National Education Association. (1996). *National directory of successful strategies for the recruitment and retention of minority teachers*. Washington, DC: Author.

Parks-Daloz, L. (1996, May 22). Education for the new commons. *Education Week*, p. 38.

Perkins, L. M. (1989). The history of Blacks in teaching: Growth and decline within the profession. In D. Warren (Ed.), *American teachers: Histories of a profession at work*. New York: Macmillan.

Pflaum, S., & Abramson, T. (1990). Teacher assignment, hiring, and preparation in New York City. *Urban Review, 22*, 12–31.

Powell, A. (1996). *Lessons from privilege*. Cambridge, MA: Harvard University Press.

Presley, C. (1991). The plunge into the White world. *Independent School, 50*(3), 27–28. (Reprint of article originally published in *Independent School* in 1971)

Richardson, J. (1995, May 17). Talent scouts. *Education Week*, pp. 22–26.

Rosenthal, R., & Jacobsen, L. F. (1968). Teacher expectations for the disadvantaged. *Scientific American, 218*(4), 19–22.

Schevtchuk-Armstrong, L. (1991, January 16). Racial, ethnic prejudice still prevalent, survey finds. *Education Week*, pp. 18–19.

Senge, P. M. (1990). *The fifth discipline: The art & practice of the learning organization*. New York: Doubleday.

Shade, B. J., & New, C. A. (1989). Cultural influences on learning: Teaching implications. In J. A. Banks & C. A. Banks (Eds.), *Multicultural education: Issues and perspectives*. Boston: Allyn & Bacon.

Sherman, T. M., Giles, M., & Williams-Green, J. (1994). Assessment and retention of Black students in higher education. *Journal of Negro Education, 63*(2), 164–179.

Simpson, A. W., & Erickson, M. T. (1983). Teachers' verbal and non-verbal communication patterns as a function of teacher race, student gender, and student race. *American Educational Research Journal, 20*(2), 183–198.

Smith, A. L. (1990). Collaborative induction model to support first year minority teachers. *Action in Teacher Education, 11*(4), 42–47.

Smith, G. P. (1987). *The effects of competency testing on the supply of minority teachers* (Report prepared for the Task Force on Teaching as a Profession). New York: Carnegie Forum on Education and the Economy.

Smith, G. P. (1988, July). A case study of the impact of performance-based testing on the supply of minority teachers. *Journal of Teacher Education, 39*(4), 45-53.

Spellman, S. O. (1988, July–August). Recruitment of minority teachers: Issues, problems, facts, possible solutions. *Journal of Teacher Education, 39*, 58-63.

Stevens, L. B. (1996, June 19). The place of race in America. *Education Week*, p. 46.

Tanner, D. E. (1986). New directions in minority teacher education. *Action in Teacher Education, 8*(1), 13-17.

Tatum, B. D. (1997). *Why are all the Black kids sitting together in the cafeteria?* New York: Basic Books.

U.S. Census Bureau. (1990). *Zip code summary file 3B*. Washington, DC: Author.

U.S. Census Bureau. (1996). *Statistical abstract of the United States*. Washington, DC: Author.

U.S. Census Bureau. (1999). *Statistical abstract of the United States*. Washington, DC: Author.

U.S. Census Bureau. (1999). *Table NPD1A: Projections of the resident population by age, sex, race and hispanic origin, 1999-2000*. Washington, DC: Author.

U.S. Census Bureau. (2002). *Statistical abstract of the United States*. Washington, DC: Author.

Walsh, M. (1991, March 13). Upper class parents support diversity, quality of public schools, study finds. *Education Week*, pp. 8-9.

Washington, V. (1980). Teachers in integrated classrooms: Profiles of attitudes, perceptions, and behavior. *Elementary School Journal, 80*, 193-201.

Wilson, Z. V. (1983). *They took their stand*. Atlanta: Mid-South Association of Independent Schools.

Witty, E. P. (1989). Increasing the pool of Black teachers: Plans and strategies. In A. M. Garibaldi (Ed.), *Teacher recruitment and retention: With a special focus on minority teachers*. Washington, DC: National Education Association.

Worner, R. B. (1991). *Minority teacher recruitment, preparation, and retention*. St. Paul: Minnesota State Department of Education, Educational Opportunities Section.

Index